While you introduce the story to the class, give the readers a moment to look over the script and identify their speaking parts and any actions they are being asked to perform. Make sure your readers know that they're not supposed to read the stage directions aloud. *(The stage directions are italicized and appear in parentheses.)* Also, the presence of an em dash (—) at the end of a sentence signifies that the speaker is being cut off mid-sentence, and the presence of an em dash at the beginning of a sentence means that reader is interrupting the other one.

In most cases, it's not crucial whether you choose a boy or a girl for a specific reading part. Sometimes it might be funny to have a girl play a part that's obviously a boy's part (such as Peter), or to have a boy play a girl's part (such as Mary Magdalene). In any case, if you reverse gender roles be sure you mention it to the audience. Children won't always know just by a name if a Bible character is male or female and you don't want the students to be confused or misinformed.

Step 6: Sit back and enjoy!

Once you're ready to begin, sit toward the front of the class with the rest of the listeners. Say, "OK, let's give our storyteller a hand and get started! . . . Lights . . . Camera . . . Action!"

Don't stay onstage with the readers while they're presenting the skit. If a director stands onstage, children often turn their backs to the audience and face the director instead. Also, you can coach and direct your readers more easily from the front row of the audience.

When the QuickSkit is finished, lead the listeners in applauding for the readers to thank them for their hard work!

WHAT KIN
THIS BOO

There are four ~~different presentation methods~~ in this collection:

1. Tandem Storytelling (*two storytellers alternate telling a story*)

When two storytellers take turns telling the same story, we say that the story is told in "tandem." Most of the stories in this book are tandem stories.

Typically the storytellers will alternate lines as the story is told. Occasionally, though, the tellers may say their lines together.

2. Storymime (*one person tells the story; the other acts it out*)

With this type of storytelling one person serves as the primary storyteller and the other person does the actions or shows the emotions of the characters and events in the story. The speaking storyteller pauses after every action verb to allow time for her partner to act out what's happening in the story. Suggested actions are included in the storymime scripts in this book.

Invite the audience to imitate, or "mime," the actions after the silent storyteller has performed them. This is a great way to include audience participation and works especially well with five- to ten-year-olds. When doing this, remember to have your reader wait long enough for the children to perform each action before reading the next section.

3. Interview (*one person interviews an eyewitness to the story*)

A few of the scripts in this book portray interviews in which a detective or reporter arrives on the scene of an important Bible event and then interviews one of the characters from the story. For this type of story, it's fun to dress the part and wear crazy costumes!

4. Sports Announcer (*both readers report as if watching the story live*)

In this style, both readers pretend to be sports announcers who are reporting live from the scene of a famous Bible event. Once again, it can be fun to dress the part and act as if you really are announcing a game on TV.

COMMON QUESTIONS

What do I need to tell the students about acting and performing?

Encourage the students to look up at the audience whenever possible during the story rather than down at the script the whole time. At first the readers might not look up at all, but their eye contact will improve the more they practice performing QuickSkits and become more comfortable reading aloud.

Tell your readers, "Remember, the audience will want to see you while you're reading, so don't turn your back on them or hold the script in front of your face."

Remind the students not to continue reading if the audience is still laughing at the previous line. Instead, wait until the laughter dies down before continuing so that all the listeners can hear the words of the story.

Explain that when you tell a story with a partner, you want the delivery to be so seamless that it feels like a unified whole rather than an awkward combination of two people's parts. To achieve this unity, readers should respond naturally and genuinely to their partner's words and actions.

Tell your readers, "As you work on your story, you'll notice that sometimes the exchange between the two storytellers is quick—each line may be only one or two words long. During these rapid-fire exchanges, be quick responding to each other, almost cutting each other off.

"And when your partner is saying her lines, don't draw attention away from the story by pacing, swaying, or fiddling with your hair or clothes."

Sometimes, one student may be a little slow in finding her lines. When that happens, the other storyteller might say something like, "Hey! Say your part!" Stop this if you see it happening. Instead, encourage your students not to interrupt or correct each other, but only to read their own lines and leave the prompting to you, the director.

As the children perform, you may wish to encourage them to act out certain parts of the story. For example,

when Peter is walking on the water and begins to sink, you could say, "OK, Peter, start sinking!" For the most part, though, encourage the readers to only perform the actions that are specifically mentioned in the scripts. Otherwise, the readers may get confused or lose their place.

Can I change the wording of the scripts in this book?

Feel free to make minor editorial changes to the scripts in this book. You may wish to leave out a joke that wouldn't make sense to your listeners or to delete a phrase that might be misunderstood. However, permission is not granted to alter the stories in such a way that you change the theological meaning or intent of the story.

Do we need special costumes or props?

A few stories include simple props. Unless otherwise noted, no special costumes are needed for the stories. In most of these stories, one of the storytellers is more serious, while the other storyteller acts somewhat goofy. If you meet regularly with the same group of students, you may wish to have the same people, dressed in memorable or distinctive costumes, tell stories as these characters. The students will look forward to seeing the funny characters again and again! If you use a puppet for one of the characters, it typically works best to have the puppet perform the role of the goofier storyteller.

Use general stage lighting and microphones if your audience is large. Make sure the listeners can hear the performers and won't be distracted by other things going on in the room.

Summary

As you present these stories, remember to encourage your students to face the audience and use plenty of facial expressions, sound effects, and natural gestures. Finally, encourage them to respond to the audience and enjoy themselves![1]

---

[1]For more extensive tips on creative storytelling, see my book *The Creative Storytelling Guide for Children's Ministry* (Standard Publishing, 2002). For additional collections of QuickSkits for kids, check out *30 Old Testament QuickSkits for Kids* (Standard Publishing, 2004) and *30 New Testament QuickSkits for Kids* (Standard Publishing, 2004).

Bible Story QuickSkits for 2 Kids

STEVEN JAMES

Standard PUBLISHING
Bringing The Word to Life

Cincinnati, Ohio

THANKS & ACKNOWLEDGMENTS

Thanks to Ruth Frederick and Paul Learned for their friendship and encouragement to think outside the box; to Dawn Korth and David Lehman for their perceptive editing; to Pamela Harty for believing in me; to Terry Maughon and the staff at Doe River Gorge Ministries for giving me a place to think, write, tell stories, and talk to my wolf; to Dana Standridge and Rhonda Bier for their tireless typing and attentive research; and to my wife and daughters for their extraordinary patience and delightful ideas.

Published by Standard Publishing, Cincinnati, Ohio
www.standardpub.com

14 13 12 11 10 09 08   7 6 5 4 3 2 1

ISBN: 978-7847-2244-2

Editorial Team: Dawn Korth, Ruth Frederick, Elaina Meyers
Creative Team: Liz Malwitz, Paula Becker, Dale Meyers

TABLE OF CONTENTS

HOW TO USE THIS BOOK

Kids love stories. They especially love listening to stories when they're told in a humorous, lively, and engaging manner. This book was designed to help you do just that. Each kid-friendly skit retells a Bible story in a fun and creative way using only two students. Best of all, the scripts are super-easy to use and aren't intimidating for students because there aren't any lines to memorize.

Just choose your story, photocopy the scripts, hand them out to your students, and you have an instant lesson.

Here are some simple steps for making the most of this book.

Step 1: Read the script.

Before class, read through the complete QuickSkit and look for any words or concepts that your children might not be familiar with. Before beginning the skit, explain the ideas taught in the skit and teach your readers how to pronounce the unusual names.

You may wish to glance through the Table of Contents, the Scripture Verse Index, or the Topical Index to find the perfect story for your group.

Step 2: Research the story.

You'll want to familiarize yourself with the Bible story so that you can answer any questions that might arise after the QuickSkit has been presented. So look the story up in the Bible and read it for yourself to make sure you understand the content and context of the material.

Please note that each QuickSkit is based on a Bible story, but has been adapted for live performance. Some stories are condensed or revised; others include only select parts of the story (so that it remains age-appropriate for children).

Step 3: Prepare the scripts.

If you have two copies of this book you can give each reader one copy to use; otherwise, you'll need to photocopy enough copies of the QuickSkit to give one copy to each of the readers (photocopy permission

is granted for this purpose). Make one extra copy for yourself so that you can follow along and help prompt a child if she can't find her part, or if she stumbles over the pronunciation of a word. You may wish to place each script in a black folder (or a different-colored folder for each reader) so that the audience doesn't see the scripts.

To avoid confusion for the readers, it's helpful to use a highlighter to identify the speaking parts for each person throughout the skit. This makes it much easier for the readers to locate their lines.

Decide whether or not you wish to use any costumes or props for the story. If you decide to use props or costumes, gather those at this time.

Step 4: Assign parts.

As you review the script, consider which of your students would best fit the different reading parts. For all the parts you'll want to choose children who are comfortable reading aloud and presenting in front of a group. Some of the characters in the skits are humorous, and their lines contain silly comments or jokes. For those parts, don't be afraid to choose kids who like to act a little goofy.

Depending upon the amount of confidence you have in the reading ability of your students, you may wish to give them the scripts before class to let them familiarize themselves with the script before performing the story in front of the rest of the group.

If you have younger children in your class (or children who aren't comfortable reading in front of others), you could use adult or teen volunteers to read the scripts instead. The reading level is targeted for 4th grade and up. If you use a puppet for one of the characters, it typically works best to have the puppet perform the role of the goofier storyteller.

Step 5: Hand out the scripts.

Now that you've familiarized yourself with the story, identified sections that might cause your students to stumble, photocopied the scripts, and chosen your readers, your pre-class preparation is done.

THE WORLD'S FIRST ARTIST
(CREATION)

BASED ON: Genesis 1, 2; Hebrews 11:3

BIG IDEA: God created the natural universe out of chaos and darkness.

BACKGROUND: The Bible opens with the account of creation. Our mighty and powerful God created the earth and the heavens and all the galaxies when he said, "Let there be."

No one knows exactly when God created the world, but believing that he did is a central teaching of the Christian faith.

Our views of the origin of the earth are not based on science, but on our faith in the Scriptures. As Hebrews 11:3 says, "By faith we understand that the universe was formed at God's command, so that what is seen was not made out of what was visible."

CAST: Bonnie—A slightly more serious storyteller trying to tell the story (girl or boy)
George—Her friend, who occasionally gets things mixed up (boy or girl)

Note: These names are used only for the purpose of clarity in the script. You may wish to use the actual names of the two storytellers as you present the story.

PROPS: A flashlight, a loaded squirt gun, and a surfboard (if desired)

TOPICS: Creation, God's existence, God's power, rest

DIRECTOR'S TIPS: This script contains a number of unusual words (such as *estuaries* and *lagoons*), so before presenting the story, make sure your readers know how to pronounce all the words.

If desired, teach the students the words of the refrain and invite them to join along whenever George repeats it throughout the story.

The readers could be either boys or girls. Both readers start onstage or enter together. Bring up the stage lights and then begin when the students are quiet.

DAY 1

Teacher: **Lights! . . . Camera! . . . Action!**

Bonnie: **Long ago—**

George: **—Before there was anything else,**

Bonnie: **There was God.**

George: **And he decided to make a very cool universe!**

Bonnie: **Now, before he created our world, it was formless—**

George: **—Like a great big glob of goo!**

Bonnie: **Right.**

George: **All gross and disgusting and slimy.**

Bonnie: **Well, something like that. And God said,**

George:	"Hmm. Looks like play dough. I think I'll make a world."
Bonnie:	Nope. Actually, he said, "Let there be light!"
George:	(Pull out a flashlight and shine it in Bonnie's eyes)
Bonnie:	Um, God didn't use a flashlight.
George:	Why not?
Bonnie:	He didn't have to. He could just use his mouth.
George:	God used his mouth as a flashlight?
Bonnie:	Don't be ridiculous. He used his mouth to say, "Let there be light!" That's all it took. And as he said it, light appeared. And after he'd made light, God said:
George:	"Let there be light bulbs! (Hold up the flashlight again) And flashlights!"
Bonnie:	No, God said, (With rhythm) "Good! Good! My light is good! It's just the way I like it, 'cause my light is good!" Try it.
George:	(With rhythm) "Good! Good! My light is good! It's just the way I like it, 'cause my light is good!"
Bonnie:	OK.
George:	"Good! Good! My light is good! It's just the way I like it, 'cause my light is good!"
Bonnie:	That's enough.
George:	"Good! Good! My light is good! It's just the way I like it, 'cause my light is good!"
Bonnie:	All right, already!
George:	That's kinda catchy.
Bonnie:	Thank you.
George:	You're welcome.
Bonnie:	Then, God called the light—
George:	"Duracell."
Bonnie:	No.
George:	"Eveready?"
Bonnie:	And together, the time of light and the time of darkness made up one day . . .
George:	"Good! Good! My day is good! It's just the way I like it, 'cause my day is good! . . . Good! Good! My flashlight's good! It's just the way I like it, 'cause my flashlight's good!"

DAY 2

Bonnie:	Now, on the second day, God pushed some water up into the sky and some down into the sea—
George:	—Did you say water?
Bonnie:	Yes . . .
George:	Oh. How nice. (Pull out a squirt gun)
Bonnie:	(Don't notice the squirt gun) And so he created the—
George:	(Squirt Bonnie) —Squirt guns!
Bonnie:	Stop that! God made the sky and the air and then God said,
George:	"Good! Good! My sky is good! It's just the way I like it, 'cause my sky is good . . . Good! Good! My squirt gun's good! It's just the way I like it, 'cause my squirt gun's good!"

DAY 3

Bonnie:	On the third day, God said, "Let's see some land!" and he gathered all the waters together in different places to make seas and rivers and oceans.
George:	(Pull out squirt gun)
Bonnie:	But not squirt guns.

George: Too bad . . . (*Squirt the audience*) **Did he make lakes and puddles and streams?**

Bonnie: Yes.

George: Ponds and rivers and brooks?

Bonnie: Uh-huh.

George: Estuaries, lagoons, and marshes?

Bonnie: What?

George: Did God make waves?

Bonnie: Well, yeah. I guess so.

George: Did he make a splash?!

Bonnie: Yes he did.

George: (*Optional: pull out a surfboard*) **And surfboards!**

Bonnie: He did not make surfboards.

George: Oh. Too bad.

Bonnie: But he did make land and he also made all kinds of plants and trees and flowers.

George: "Good! Good! My plants are good! They're just the way I like 'em, 'cause my plants are good!" (*Jump on surfboard*) "Good! Good! The surfing's good! It's just the way I like it, 'cause the surfing's good!"

DAY 4

Bonnie: Then on the fourth day, God made the sun and the moon and the stars and the planets in the sky. And God made the moon to shine at night and the sun to shine during the—

George: (*Interrupting*) —Wait a minute, if he didn't make the sun 'til day four, how could there be day and night on day one and two and three?

Bonnie: Well, remember, he already had light and darkness. He knew what a day was. He just hadn't put the light in a sun or a star yet.

George: But how could that be? How could he do that?

Bonnie: He's God.

George: Oh, yeah. Right. "Good! Good! My stars are good! They're just the way I like 'em, 'cause my stars are good!"

DAY 5

Bonnie: On the fifth day, God made fish and eels and dolphins and sharks—

George: —And sea monsters! (*Yelling*) Aaahhhh!

Bonnie: Not sea monsters, but sea turtles; and then God made the birds.

George: Cawk! Cawk!

Bonnie: Right!

George: And God said, "Good! Good! My fishies are good! They're just the way I like 'em, 'cause my fishies are good!"

Bonnie: Right!

George: "Good! Good! My birdies are good! They're just the way I like 'em, 'cause my birdies are good!"

Bonnie: You got it!

George: "Good! Good! My sea monsters are good! They're just the way I like 'em, 'cause my sea monsters are good!"

DAY 6

Bonnie: On the sixth day, God made cows and horses and pigs and—

George: —Werewolves.

Bonnie: There were no werewolves!

George: Vampires! (*Talking like a vampire*) I vant to suck your blood!

Bonnie: Would you stop that already?

The World's First Artist

George:	OK.
Bonnie:	God made the land animals—and people too.
George:	And the bogeyman.
Bonnie:	God did not create the bogeyman!
George:	Oh yeah? Well, who did?
Bonnie:	Nobody. There aren't such things as bogeymen.
George:	Oh. "Good! Good! My animals are good! They're just the way I like 'em, 'cause my animals are good! . . . Good! Good! My werewolves are good. They're just the way I like 'em, 'cause my werewolves are good!"
Bonnie:	Not the werewolves. People.
George:	Good! Good! My bogeyman's good—
Bonnie:	—No-no-no-no. "Good! Good! My people are good! They're just the way I like 'em, 'cause my people are good!"
George:	Right. And so is my bogeyman.

DAY 7

Bonnie:	Finally, on the seventh day,
George:	God slept in.
Bonnie:	Well, kind of.
George:	He did?
Bonnie:	Well, he rested on that day.
George:	He took a nap.
Bonnie:	Well, sort of.
George:	All that creating tired him out, huh?
Bonnie:	No. God doesn't get tired.
George:	Then why'd he sleep in on the seventh day? Huh? Huh? Huh?

Bonnie:	He didn't sleep. He rested on that day so he could enjoy all that he'd made. And he called it the most special day of all because—
George:	There was no school!
Bonnie:	Um, not exactly. It was a day set apart for renewal and enjoyment and rest from our work.
George:	And from school.
Bonnie:	Well, yeah.
George:	Cool . . . "Good! Good! My rest is good! It's just the way I like it 'cause my rest is good!"
Bonnie:	So, just like a painter, God first made sure he had enough light. Then, he got the canvas ready.
George:	By separating the waters from the sky?
Bonnie:	That's right.
George:	And making the dry land and the oceans?
Bonnie:	Uh-huh. And then, he started adding color.
George:	Oh, with trees and plants and flowers!
Bonnie:	Right! And then he filled the sky with lights: Stars and the moon and the sun so the background for his masterpiece would look just right.
George:	And then came the details!
Bonnie:	Yes! He filled his canvas with the best products of his imagination.
George:	Sea monsters and werewolves!
Bonnie:	Um, no.
George:	Fish and birds?
Bonnie:	Yeah, and then the land animals.
George:	Wow!
Bonnie:	And people.

George:	And bogeymen.	Together:	"Good! Good! My world is good! It's just the way I like it, 'cause my world is good!"
Bonnie:	And finally, he put the finishing touches on his masterpiece and stepped back to admire it.	Together:	The end.
George:	"Cool."		
Bonnie:	Actually he said,		

(Bow. Fade out the stage lights. As the storytellers exit, George sings, "Good! Good! My sea monsters are good! They're just the way I like 'em, 'cause my sea monsters are good!")

THE DAY SIN CAME IN
(THE GARDEN OF EDEN)

BASED ON: Genesis 3

BIG IDEA: Adam and Eve chose to disobey God, and because of their choice, sin entered the world. Yet through it all, God still showed them compassion and grace.

BACKGROUND: Sometimes when people read the story of Adam and Eve, they think God wasn't fair in how he treated his newly created people. Why would he create a tree that could cause them death? Why didn't he just overlook their one "little mistake?" And why did he call out for them; couldn't he tell where they were? This script addresses some of these questions and demonstrates that God continued to treat his children with justice, mercy, love, and compassion.

CAST: Bonnie—A slightly more serious storyteller trying to tell the story (girl or boy)
George—Her friend, who occasionally gets things mixed up (boy or girl)

Note: These names are used only for the purpose of clarity in the script. You may wish to use the actual names of the two storytellers as you present the story.

PROPS: None

TOPICS: Choices, consequences, death, excuses, forgiveness, God's love, grace, obedience, second chances, sin, temptation

DIRECTOR'S TIPS: During parts of this story, George sings his own version of lines from the song "Do-Re-Mi" from *The Sound of Music*. Make sure he's familiar with these phrases and with the tune before beginning the story.

The storytellers could be either boys or girls. Both readers start onstage or enter together. Bring up the stage lights and then begin when the students are quiet.

Teacher: **Lights! . . . Camera! . . . Action!**

Bonnie: **Today, we have a really exciting story to tell you.**

George: **It's a story about Adam.**

Bonnie: **And Eve.**

George: **And a choice they made long ago,**

Bonnie: **In the Garden of Eden. Now, the snake,**

George: *(Emphasizing the "s" sounds)* **SSSSSSSSSSSSSSSSSSS—was the s-s-s-sneakiest, s-s-s-slitheries-s-s-st, creature in all of God's-s-s-s garden.**

Bonnie: **And one day, he went into the branches of a tree in the middle of the garden; a tree that God had told Adam and Eve not to eat from.**

George: *(As the snake)* **"S-s-s-so, Eve, did God really s-s-say you shouldn't eat anything in this-s-s-s whole garden?"**

Bonnie: *(As Eve)* "Of course not! We can eat stuff, but not the fruit from this tree. If we even touch it we'll die.

George: *(As a storyteller again, to Bonnie)* Wait. Did God really say that?

Bonnie: No. God's rule was they couldn't eat it.

George: So, why'd she say they couldn't touch it?

Bonnie: She was adding to what God said. And that was her first mistake.

George: I thought her first mistake was listening to a talking snake. I mean, Hello, lady! Are snakes supposed to talk? I don't think so.

Bonnie: Let's get back to the story.

George: *(As the tempter again)* "You won't die! You'll become like God. You'll know all about what's-s-s-s good and what's-s-s-s evil."

Bonnie: Eve looked at the tree.

George: She listened to the snake.

Bonnie: She reached out her hand and—

George: —Wait a minute!

Bonnie: What?

George: What's she doing?

Bonnie: She's gonna eat the fruit.

George: But why?

Bonnie: The snake convinced her. And the fruit looked fresh and sweet and yummy. And she thought it would make her smarter.

George: But God told her not to!

Bonnie: Uh-huh.

George: And she was gonna do it anyway?

Bonnie: Uh-huh.

George: So what about Adam? Where was he during all this?

Bonnie: He was standing right beside her.

George: What? Why didn't he stop her? He heard the whole snake thing and he didn't do anything to stop his wife?

Bonnie: That's right.

George: Wow! Now there's a world-class leader.

Bonnie: Eve reached out her hand and picked some of the fruit.

George: *(Dramatically)* Oh, no! I can't watch!

Bonnie: She lifted it to her mouth—

George: —Don't do it, Eve! Don't do it! You're gonna die! Put it back! Stick it on a branch like a Christmas tree ornament or something! *(Take a piece of imaginary fruit from Eve's hand and stick it onto an imaginary tree.)*

Bonnie: She opened her mouth—

George: —And decided not to eat the fruit after all. She put it in a fruit bowl on her dining room table, and lived happily ever after with her hard-working but somewhat dim-witted husband, Adam.

Bonnie: What? That's not how it goes.

George: So she threw it to the ground and said, "I shall not eateth of this fruiteth, for the Lord hath commandedeth me not to eateth . . . of iteth."

Bonnie: Nope.

George: But can't we stop her? Isn't there anything we can do?

Bonnie: Nope. She bit into the fruit, and she liked it so much, she gave some to Adam. And he—

George: —Put her on a timeout.

Bonnie: No. He ate the fruit too.

George: Oh, no! They're gonna die! They're probably gonna choke on it or something. Do they die?

Bonnie:	Not right away.
George:	But God told them they would, right?
Bonnie:	Yeah. And he always keeps his promises.
George:	But then why didn't they die?
Bonnie:	They did eventually, but because God loved them so much, he let them stay alive for a long time.
George:	Wow. Cool.
Bonnie:	At that moment, when they ate the fruit, they realized they were naked.
George:	What? AAAAHHHHH! *(Throw your arms across your body, as if you were standing there with no clothes on)* You mean they weren't wearing any clothes?!
Bonnie:	That's right.
George:	Yowsa. *(Stop covering yourself and stand normal again)*
Bonnie:	Clothes hadn't been invented yet. And neither had bellybuttons.
George:	Huh?
Bonnie:	Never mind. And they felt ashamed of themselves.
George:	No kidding. I'd be ashamed too, if I was walking around naked without a bellybutton and eating a bunch of fruit with talking reptiles.
Bonnie:	The shame came from disobeying God. Before that, they didn't need clothes. So they sewed some fig leaves together for their clothes.
George:	Where'd they get the sewing machine from?
Bonnie:	They didn't use a sewing machine.
George:	So . . . a needle pulling thread?
Bonnie:	Right.

George:	*(Singing)* Blah, their clothes were not so good!
Bonnie:	And that night, God came looking for them for—
George:	*(Singing)* —Tea, a drink with jam and bread.
Bonnie:	But they ran from God.
George:	*(Singing)* Fa, a long, long way to run!
Bonnie:	Um . . .
George:	But why did they run?
Bonnie:	Shame. They were still ashamed. Then God called, "Adam! Where are you?"
George:	*(Singing)* Me, I'm hiding by the tree . . . *(Talking)* Wait a minute. God couldn't find 'em?
Bonnie:	Of course he could. He's God.
George:	Hmm. I'll bet he was giving them a chance to step out and admit their mistake, wasn't he?
Bonnie:	I think you're right. So, finally Adam said to God, "I was scared when I heard you because I was naked!"
George:	*(Act ashamed that you are naked again)*
Bonnie:	So they were scared, ashamed, hiding,
George:	And naked.
Bonnie:	Right. And that's how we still feel today when we do something wrong.
George:	We feel naked?
Bonnie:	No, but all the other stuff though.
George:	Oh. And when God talked to them about it, Adam blamed Eve and Eve blamed the talking snake.
Bonnie:	God cursed the snake and promised that a child born of a woman would crush the snake, even though the child would be wounded in the process.

The Day Sin Came In

George: Wait a minute! . . . That snake wasn't just any old ordinary snake, was he? He was really the devil in disguise. Right?

Bonnie: Right. And who crushed the power of the devil?

George: Jesus!

Bonnie: Right.

George: So, God gave Adam and Eve a promise to believe in,

Bonnie: And he gave us a promise to believe in too.

George: Right. A promise of forgiveness through Jesus,

Bonnie: The one who crushes sin and conquers death.

George: So we can be forgiven without having to walk around naked!

Bonnie: And that's a good thing.

Together: The end.

(Bow. Fade out the stage lights. Exit.)

THE FLOOD (NOAH)

BASED ON: Genesis 6–9

BIG IDEA: Even though the world around him was evil, Noah trusted in God and obeyed him. As a result, God rescued Noah and his family from destruction.

BACKGROUND: As the population on earth grew, great wickedness spread among the people (Genesis 6:5). Seeing so much sin in the world broke God's heart, so he decided to send a great flood and wipe out the whole human race. But Noah followed God and had a close relationship with Him. God chose to rescue Noah and his family as well as representatives from the different species of animals from the devastating worldwide flood.

CAST: Bonnie—A slightly more serious storyteller trying to tell the story (girl or boy)
George—Her friend, who occasionally gets things mixed up (boy or girl)

Note: These names are used only for the purpose of clarity in the script. You may wish to use the actual names of the two storytellers as you present the story.

PROPS: A leafy branch

TOPICS: Consequences, faith, following God, God's power, obedience, rebellion, second chances, sin

DIRECTOR'S TIPS: Place the leafy branch in the back of the room before the story begins. The readers could be either boys or girls. Both readers start onstage or enter together. Bring up the stage lights and then begin when the students are quiet.

Teacher: **Lights! . . . Camera! . . . Action!**

Bonnie: **Long ago when the earth was young,**

George: **The people turned away from God.**

Bonnie: **The world was filled with mean,**

George: **Cruel,**

Bonnie: **Nasty,**

George: **Rotten,**

Bonnie: **No good,**

George: **Naughty, naughty,**

Bonnie: **Really bad people.**

George: **But there was one guy who followed the Lord.**

Bonnie: **And his name was Noah.**

George: **One day, God told him,**

Bonnie: **"Noah, the world is filled with mean,**

George: **Cruel,**

Bonnie: **Nasty,**

George: **Rotten,**

Bonnie: **No good,**

George: **Naughty, naughty,**

Bonnie: **Really bad people. So I've decided to start over."**

George: **Oh.**

Bonnie: **"With you."**

George: **Whoa.**

Bonnie: **"So build a boat big enough for your whole family and two of every kind of animal in the whole wide world."**

George: **All right, if you say so.**

Bonnie: **"I do."**

George: **Gotcha.**

Bonnie: **So, Noah hammered and sawed and hammered and sawed until—**

George: **His arm was really tired,**

Bonnie: **And his boat was really done.**

George: **Then, God told him to get into the boat with his family.**

Bonnie: **And a week later,**

George: **The rains came down,**

Bonnie: **And the floods came up.**

George: **And the lifeguards dove in.**

Bonnie: **There were no lifeguards.**

George: **Then who dove in to save all the people who weren't in the boat?**

Bonnie: **No one did. They didn't survive.**

George: **Oh.**

Bonnie: **And so all those mean,**

George: **Cruel,**

Bonnie: **Nasty,**

George: **Rotten,**

Bonnie: **No good,**

George: **Naughty, naughty,**

Bonnie: **Really bad people were washed away and drowned in the flood.**

George: **The sky split open and rain came crashing down.**

Bonnie: **Thunder rolled across the heavens.**

George: **And even the earth burst open and shot water into the air.**

Bonnie: **Waters came from high in the sky,**

George: **And down in the earth,**

Bonnie: **And the boat rose higher and higher on the waves.**

George: **But Noah and his family,**

Bonnie: **And all those animals were safe inside the boat.**

George: **Inside, there were two cows.**

Bonnie: *(As George lists the animals, make the appropriate sound effects)* **Moo! Moo!**

George: **Two snakes.**

Bonnie: **Hiss! Hiss!**

George: **Two hippos.**

Bonnie: **Blub. Blub.**

George: **Two worms.**

Bonnie: **Squiggle. Squiggle.**

George: **Two octopuses.**

Bonnie: **Um—**

George: **Two sharks.**

Bonnie: **Wait a minute.**

The Flood

George: A couple of eels.

Bonnie: No, no, no.

George: And two blue whales.

Bonnie: The whales and sharks and eels weren't on the boat. They were in the water.

George: Oh. Eating all the dead people, I suppose.

Bonnie: That's gross! Look, the rain fell for forty days,

George: And forty nights.

Bonnie: But Noah,

George: And his wife,

Bonnie: And his three sons,

George: And their wives,

Bonnie: Were safe and sound inside the boat.

George: With all those snakes.

Bonnie: Hiss! Hiss!

George: Hippos.

Bonnie: Blub. Blub.

George: Worms.

Bonnie: Squiggle. Squiggle.

George: Octopuses.

Bonnie: Isn't that supposed to be octopi?

George: No thanks, I'm not hungry.

Bonnie: Wait a minute—

George: —Sharks, eels, and whales.

Bonnie: And, finally, the water covered the whole earth.

George: Even the highest mountains.

Bonnie: The water covered the earth for 150 days.

George: That's a long time to be shut up in a boat with a bunch of—

Bonnie: —Oh, no, not again.

George: Oh, yeah. Cows,

Bonnie: Moo. Moo.

George: And snakes.

Bonnie: Hiss. Hiss.

George: And hippos.

Bonnie: Blub. Blub.

George: And worms.

Bonnie: Squiggle. Squiggle.

George: Right! And God remembered Noah and his family and all those animals.

Bonnie: And he sent a strong wind.

George: WHOOSH! (Blow in Bonnie's face)

Bonnie: (Cough as if George has bad breath)

George: And the waters began to evaporate—Whoosh!

Bonnie: The boat stopped floating and landed on the top of Mount Ararat. And then, after many days, Noah opened the door and sent out a dove.

George: (Flap your arms like wings)

Bonnie: (Stare at George) Apparently it was a rather big dove . . .

George: (Fly around the audience and then come back on stage)

Bonnie: (Wait for George to return to the stage before talking) But the dove couldn't find a place to land because the water was still too high. Noah reached out his arm and the dove landed on it. (Stick out your arm)

George:	*(Look at Bonnie's arm, then at the audience, and try to jump on her arm)*
Bonnie:	**A week later, he sent out the dove again.**
George:	*(Flap your arms like wings and fly around the audience again)*
Bonnie:	**Toward evening, the dove returned with an olive branch in his beak.**
George:	*(Grab the leafy branch from the back of the room and carry it up in your hand)*
Bonnie:	**Um, I said "in his beak," not "in his wing."**
George:	*(Stick it in your mouth and keep flapping your arms in front of the audience)*
Bonnie:	**A week later, he sent out the dove again.**
George:	*(Fly off again)*
Bonnie:	**This time, the dove did not return.**
George:	*(Go out the door, out of the room)*
Bonnie:	*(Yelling)* **But the storyteller did return!**
George:	*(Open the door, peek your head in)* **Oh, OK.** *(Come back onstage)*
Bonnie:	**Finally, twelve-and-a-half months after the flood began, Noah and his family left the boat and brought with them all of those cows—**
George:	*(Don't do anything)*

Bonnie:	**What are you waiting for?**
George:	**I don't do the animal sounds. That's your part.**
Bonnie:	**Oh, c'mon, please?**
George:	*(Shake your head "no")*
Bonnie:	*(Sighing)* **Oh, all right.**
George:	**The cows!**
Bonnie:	*(Make all the animal sounds reluctantly)* **Moo. Moo.**
George:	**And snakes.**
Bonnie:	**Hiss. Hiss.**
George:	**And hippos.**
Bonnie:	**Blub. Blub.**
George:	**And worms.**
Bonnie:	**Squiggle. Squiggle.**
George:	**And the rest of the animals.**
Bonnie:	**Noah and his family worshiped God,**
George:	**And then God sent a beautiful rainbow as a reminder that he would never again send a flood across the whole wide world.**
Together:	**The end.**

(Bow. Fade out the stage lights. Exit.)

The Flood

THE GUY WHO WOULDN'T KISS MRS. POTTY (JOSEPH—PART 1)

BASED ON: Genesis 37, 39

BIG IDEA: Joseph continued to trust that God would work everything out for good even when bad things happened throughout his life.

BACKGROUND: Jacob showed favoritism to his son, Joseph. Eventually Joseph's brothers began to hate and resent him. In the end, they faked his death, sold him as a slave, and lied to their father to cover it all up. Then, through a series of divinely orchestrated circumstances, Joseph became second-in-charge of Egypt. Eventually, Joseph and his brothers became reunited and he forgave them for what they'd done to him.

In this skit, the first of three stories about Joseph's life, Joseph ends up in an Egyptian jail after being falsely accused of wrongdoing.

Since the story of Joseph's life takes up such a large chunk of the Bible, it would be tough to cover the whole story in one lesson. This script covers only one part of Joseph's life. You'll want to make sure the children don't think this Joseph is the same man who was married to Jesus' mother.

CAST: Bonnie—A slightly more serious storyteller trying to tell the story (girl or boy)
George—Her friend, who occasionally gets things mixed up (boy or girl)

Note: These names are used only for the purpose of clarity in the script. You may wish to use the actual names of the two storytellers as you present the story.

PROPS: None

TOPICS: Bullies, courage, family relationships, God's love, jealousy, questions, resentment, suffering

DIRECTOR'S TIPS: This script contains a number of unusual words (such as *mauve*), and names (such as *Bilhah* and *Zilpah*), so before presenting the story, make sure your readers know how to pronounce all the words.

The storytellers could be either boys or girls. Both readers start onstage or enter together. Bring up the stage lights and then begin when the students are quiet.

Teacher:	**Lights! . . . Camera! . . . Action!**
George:	**Today, we'd like to tell you a story of a man who went from riches,**
Bonnie:	**To rags,**
George:	**To riches,**
Bonnie:	**To rags,**
George:	**To riches.**

Bonnie:	It has adventure!
George:	Ooh!
Bonnie:	Intrigue!
George:	Ahhh!
Bonnie:	Romance!
George:	Hubba, hubba!
Bonnie:	Betrayal!
George:	*(Gasp!)*
Bonnie:	Good guys!
George:	*(Thumbs up)* Dude.
Bonnie:	Bad guys!
George:	*(Act stupid)* Duh, I'm a bad guy. See how scary I am: Grr.
Bonnie:	Fight scenes!
George:	*(Do karate moves)* Hi-ya-ka-bung-ah! Wait a minute! This story doesn't have fight scenes . . .
Bonnie:	Oops . . . Adventure!
George:	Um, you already said adventure.
Bonnie:	Oh, yeah . . . Egyptians!
George:	*(Pose like an Egyptian hieroglyph)*
Bonnie:	Lies!
George:	I'm a Bohemian gypsy tightrope walker with blue hair.
Bonnie:	And a happy ending!
George:	Aw . . . how sweet.
Bonnie:	So, let's get started. Once upon a time, there was a boy named Joseph. He lived with his dad, Jacob; his mom, Rachel; his step-mom, Leah; his other step-mom, Bilhah; and his other . . . other step-mom, Zilpah.
George:	He had three step-moms?

Bonnie:	Uh-huh.
George:	And two of 'em were named Bilhah and Zilpah?
Bonnie:	Uh-huh.
George:	Whoa. That's really unfortunate.
Bonnie:	And last but not least, he lived with his eleven brothers.
George:	Eleven brothers?
Bonnie:	Yup.
George:	It was one big, happy family.
Bonnie:	Well, you got two out of three right.
George:	What do you mean?
Bonnie:	It was big, and it was a family, but they were definitely not happy. Those eleven brothers hated Joseph because he was their dad's favorite.
George:	And one day, their dad bought him this really cool coat of many colors—purple, red, pink, orange, blue, and mauve.
Bonnie:	And his brothers decided to kill Joseph.
George:	Because of a plaid windbreaker?
Bonnie:	No, because they were jealous and they hated him. So one day, Joseph went out to visit his brothers, and they decided to kill him.
George:	By dropping him in a pit and leaving him there to die.
Bonnie:	But then, one of the brothers said, "Let's not actually kill the little twerp; let's just sell him as a slave instead."
George:	*(Sarcastically)* How kind.
Bonnie:	Yeah, well, the other brothers went for it, and they took his coat, killed a goat, and put the goat's blood on the coat.
George:	They killed a goat, and put the blood on the coat?

The Guy Who Wouldn't Kiss Mrs. Potty

Bonnie: **Right.**

George: **They coated the coat with the blood of the goat?**

Bonnie: **Uh-huh.**

George: **It was a coated goat coat?**

Bonnie: **Yes.**

George: **Take note. They took a vote and they toted the coat. Then they coated the coat with the blood of the goat.**

Bonnie: **Say what?**

George: **Lemme ask you a question.**

Bonnie: **What's that?**

George: **Were any of his brothers named Dr. Seuss?**

Bonnie: **No. And when his dad saw the bloody coat, he thought Joseph was dead.**

George: **But he wasn't dead at all.**

Bonnie: **No he wasn't. The people who bought him finally sold him as a slave to this guy in Egypt, named Potiphar.**

George: **Can we call him Mr. Potty for short?**

Bonnie: **That would be a no.**

George: **Too bad.**

Bonnie: **And Joseph was in charge of—**

George: **—Mr. Potty's house.**

Bonnie: **Don't call him Mr. Potty. It's Potiphar. And one day his wife saw Joseph and thought he was cute.**

George: **Can we call her Mrs. Potty?**

Bonnie: **Would you stop that already? And she kept coming up to him, hoping for a great big smooch.**

George: **Kissy, kissy, kissy.**

Bonnie: **But Joseph wouldn't do it, because she was already married—**

George: **—To Mr. Potty.**

Bonnie: **And God had trained Joseph never to kiss someone else's wife.**

George: **He was potty trained.**

Bonnie: **The lady was like, "My husband is gone! This is our big chance! Let's go make out!" And Joe said,**

George: **"No, way! I'm outta here!"**

Bonnie: **Right. And as he ran off,**

George: **Since he wouldn't make out with her, she pulled off his shirt and decided to get him in trouble.**

Bonnie: **So she started yelling for help.**

George: **And when her husband came,**

Bonnie: **She told him Joseph had tried to attack her.**

George: **So Mr. Potty was furious at Joseph and threw him in prison.**

Bonnie: **That's right. And even though that's not the end of Joseph's story, it is the end our story for right now.**

George: **Joseph knew he shouldn't kiss Mrs. Potty, so he didn't do it. He shows us it's always important to stand up for what you believe in.**

Bonnie: **Even if you have to stand alone.**

George: **And lesson number two,**

Bonnie: **There's a lesson number two?**

George: **Yeah. Never name your kids "Potiphar," or they're gonna have the worst nickname in the world.**

Bonnie: **You can say that again.**

Together: **The end.**

(Bow. Fade out the stage lights. Exit.)

The Guy Who Wouldn't Kiss Mrs. Potty

DUNGEON OF DREAMS

(JOSEPH—PART 2)

BASED ON: Genesis 40, 41

BIG IDEA: Joseph patiently remained faithful to God and to his convictions. We need to remain faithful to God as well.

BACKGROUND: After Potiphar sent Joseph to prison, God helped Joseph interpret the dreams of a waiter and a baker. Three years later, Joseph also interpreted Pharaoh's dream and was promoted to second-in-command of all of Egypt.

Since the story of Joseph's life takes up such a large chunk of the Bible, it would be tough to cover the whole story in one lesson. This script covers only a portion of Joseph's life. You'll want to make sure the children don't think this Joseph is the same man who was married to Jesus' mother.

CAST: Bonnie—A slightly more serious storyteller trying to tell the story (girl or boy)
George—Her friend, who occasionally gets things mixed up (boy or girl)

Note: These names are used only for the purpose of clarity in the script. You may wish to use the actual names of the two storytellers as you present the story.

PROPS: None

TOPICS: Dreams, faith, God's sovereignty, patience, purpose, suffering

DIRECTOR'S TIPS: This script contains some unusual names, such as *Zaphenath-paneah,* so before presenting the story, make sure your readers know how to pronounce all the words.

This is the continuing saga of Joseph and his rise to power in Egypt. If this skit is used separately from the previous skit, you may need to tell the students some of the background about Joseph's situation before you begin this story.

The storytellers could be either boys or girls. Both readers start onstage or enter together. Bring up the stage lights and then begin when the students are quiet.

Teacher: **Lights! . . . Camera! . . . Action!**

Bonnie: **As you may remember, Joseph had been thrown in an Egyptian prison,**

George: **Even though he hadn't done anything wrong.**

Bonnie: **Well, there were two other guys with him in prison. The royal baker, and the royal waiter.**

George: **The royal waiter? What was he doing there?**

Bonnie: **Waiting.**

George: **How appropriate.**

Bonnie: **Normally he would serve the king, but now he was waiting and hoping to get out of prison.**

George: **Which prison was it?**

Bonnie:	The one in Mr. Potiphar's palace.
George:	The one in Mr. Potty's palace.
Bonnie:	*(Sigh)* And Joseph had been put in charge of the other prisoners.
George:	Because the Lord was with him wherever he went.
Bonnie:	One night, both the waiter and the baker had a dream. And in the morning, Joseph noticed that they were both upset.
George:	"What's wrong with you guys? Why the long faces?"
Bonnie:	"We dreamed some dreams and don't know what they mean!"
George:	"God can interpret dreams. Tell me what they were about!"
Bonnie:	The waiter went first: "I saw a vine with three branches, covered with grapes. I squeezed the grapes into the king's cup. What does it mean?"
George:	"Aha! Three branches means three days! So, three days from now, you'll get your old job back! But first, you have to wait three days." *(Narrating)* And they guy was like, "That's cool. I can wait."
Bonnie:	Why would he say it was cool to wait?
George:	He was a waiter, wasn't he?
Bonnie:	And Joseph told him,
George:	"When you get back to the king's palace, promise to tell him that I'm innocent."
Bonnie:	"I promise." Now, when the baker heard what Joseph told the waiter,
George:	He was excited.
Bonnie:	"Wow! Let me tell you about my dream, too!"
George:	"Go ahead."

Bonnie:	"OK . . . In my dream, there were three baskets of pastries on my head. And the birds came and ate the ones off the top."
George:	"Three baskets means three days!"
Bonnie:	*(Excitedly)* "Yeah?"
George:	"In three days—"
Bonnie:	*(More excitedly)* "Yeah, yeah?"
George:	"The king's gonna bring you back to the palace—"
Bonnie:	*(Very excitedly)* "Uh-huh, uh-huh, go on!"
George:	"Chop off your head, stick your body on a long, pointy pole and the birds are going to come by and eat your rotting, stinking flesh."
Bonnie:	*(As Bonnie, not the baker)* Did you just say the king was going to chop off the guy's head, stick his body on a long, pointy pole and the birds were going to come by and eat his rotting, stinking flesh?
George:	Yup. Cool, huh?
Bonnie:	Disgusting. So the guy said, "Couldn't I just get my old job back like the waiter?"
George:	"Nope. You're stuck with the pointy pole and the hungry birds."
Bonnie:	So three days later, on the king's birthday, just as Joseph had predicted, the king gave the waiter his old job back, and then he took the baker—
George:	—And chopped off his head, stuck his body on a long, pointy pole and the birds came by and ate his rotting, stinking flesh.
Bonnie:	You are very gross. You know that?
George:	Thank you.
Bonnie:	But when the waiter got his old job back, he forgot all about Joseph for the next two years.
George:	Joseph waited.

Bonnie: And waited . . .

George: And waited. Even though he wasn't the waiter, he waited for the waiter to stop waiting.

Bonnie: Then one night, while the king was asleep,

George: *(Snore loudly)*

Bonnie: He had a dream. And in his dream, seven big fat cows,

George: *(Mooing loudly)* MOO! MOO!

Bonnie: Got eaten by seven scrawny, little skinny cows.

George: *(Softly)* Moo. Moo.

Bonnie: Then, the king woke up.

George: Holy cow!

Bonnie: Right. Then, he fell back asleep.

George: *(Snore loudly)*

Bonnie: And he had another dream, and this time he dreamed of seven stalks of grain.

George: What, was he hungry for breakfast or something?

Bonnie: No. Just listen.

George: OK.

Bonnie: There were seven big plump kernels of grain growing on one stalk.

George: *(Loudly)* YUMMY! YUMMY!

Bonnie: And seven skinny dry ones on another stalk.

George: *(Softly)* Yummy. Yummy.

Bonnie: And the little ones ate up the big ones.

George: The grain ate the grain?

Bonnie: Yes.

George: Which grew mainly on the plain?

Bonnie: No.

George: In the rain, in Spain?

Bonnie: No!

George: How do you know?

Bonnie: Because I can use my brain! Oh, no! Now, you've got me doing it!

George: Yeah baby. That's what I'm talking about.

Bonnie: So the king called in his magicians and his wisest advisors but all of them were clueless and didn't know what the dreams meant.

George: *(Sounding stupid)* "Duh, we don't know!"

Bonnie: *(As the king)* "Are you sure?"

George: *(Still sounding stupid)* "Duh. Uh-huh. We're totally clueless."

Bonnie: So, finally, the waiter remembered Joseph.

George: It's about time.

Bonnie: They called him up from prison to see if he could decipher the dreams of the cows,

George: MOO.

Bonnie: And the grain.

George: YUMMY.

Bonnie: The king waited while Joseph took a quick shower and changed clothes and then he told him, "Explain my dreams!"

George: "I can't."

Bonnie: "What do you mean? I thought you could tell what dreams mean!"

George: "Nope. Not me. But God can. Tell me about your dreams and God will explain their meaning to me."

Bonnie: And so the king told him all about the fat cows,

George: MOO!

Dungeon of Dreams

Bonnie:	And the skinny cows,
George:	*(Softly)* Moo.
Bonnie:	The fat grain,
George:	YUMMY!
Bonnie:	And the skinny grain,
George:	*(Softly)* Yummy.
Bonnie:	And how the skinny cows ate the fat and juicy,
George:	Hamburgers.
Bonnie:	And how the skinny grain ate up the big, plump,
George:	Whole grain buns. Tasty and nutritious.
Bonnie:	Then Joseph said,
George:	"Both dreams mean the same thing."
Bonnie:	"What's that?"
George:	"You're hungry for lunch!"
Bonnie:	*(Whispering to George)* That's not how the story goes.
George:	Oh, right . . . "Your dreams mean there are going to be seven years of lots of crops and big juicy cows."
Bonnie:	"Cool!"
George:	"And seven years of no rain, no crops, no cows, and no cereal."
Bonnie:	"Bummer."
George:	"And since you had the dream twice, it means God is totally serious about doing it and he's gonna do it really soon."
Bonnie:	"Yikes."
George:	"So you'd better find someone who knows what he's doing and put him in charge of gathering and storing food over the next seven years. That way, there'll be plenty of leftovers when the rough times come."
Bonnie:	"Good idea."
George:	"Thank you."
Bonnie:	"You've got the job."
George:	"Right on."
Bonnie:	It was a really important job, so the king gave Joseph a new set of clothes, a cool new ring, a gold chain and a brand new—
George:	Hummer.
Bonnie:	Chariot. And then he gave him a new name.
George:	What's that?
Bonnie:	Zaph-enath-paneah.
George:	You've gotta be kidding me.
Bonnie:	Nope.
George:	Zaffa . . . Zappenheimer . . . Zappapaffa . . . um, let's call him Zappo for short.
Bonnie:	Joseph—
George:	—Zappo.
Bonnie:	Was thirty years old when he was given the job.
George:	And he went right to work, gathering up food for the years without crops or rain.
Bonnie:	So in our story today, Joseph trusted God and waited for justice,
George:	And even though God took his time,
Bonnie:	Joseph never gave up on God. We need to continue to trust in God, too, when bad things happen.
George:	So, is that the end?
Bonnie:	No, there's more to the story.
George:	And we'll learn all about it next time,
Bonnie:	When we hear more of the adventures of,

George: **Zappo-man!**

Bonnie: **Joseph.**

George: **Until next time.**

Together: **The end.**

(Bow. Fade out the stage lights. Exit.)

FINAL FORGIVENESS

(JOSEPH—PART 3)

BASED ON:	Genesis 42-45, 50
BIG IDEA:	Joseph welcomed his family and forgave his brothers, even though they had hurt him. We can learn from his example and be forgiving too.
BACKGROUND:	While leading Egypt's food collection program, Joseph recognized his brothers who came to purchase food for their family. After a series of tests, Joseph revealed his identity to them, the family was reunited, and everyone learned that God can grow something good even out of our evil choices.
	Since the story of Joseph's life takes up such a large chunk of the Bible, it would be tough to cover the whole story in one lesson. This script covers only one period of Joseph's life. You'll want to make sure the children don't think this Joseph is the same man who was married to Jesus' mother.
CAST:	Bonnie—A slightly more serious storyteller trying to tell the story (girl or boy)
	George—Her friend, who occasionally gets things mixed up (boy or girl)
	Note: These names are used only for the purpose of clarity in the script. You may wish to use the actual names of the two storytellers as you present the story.
PROPS:	None
TOPICS:	Family relationships, forgiveness, God's sovereignty, leadership, suffering
DIRECTOR'S TIPS:	This is the continuing saga of Joseph and his rise to power in Egypt. If this skit is used separately from the previous two, you may need to tell the students some of the background about Joseph's situation before you begin this story.
	The storytellers could be either boys or girls. Both readers start onstage or enter together. Bring up the stage lights and then begin when the students are quiet.

Teacher: **Lights! . . . Camera! . . . Action!**

Bonnie: **So, just to remind everyone, Joseph was this rich kid.**

George: **That was good!**

Bonnie: **Who had eleven brothers who all hated his guts and wanted him dead.**

George: **That was bad.**

Bonnie: **But at the last minute, they decided to spare his life . . .**

George: **That was good!**

Bonnie: **And they sold him as a slave.**

George: **That was bad.**

Bonnie: **He was put in charge of a rich guy's house in Egypt!**

George: That was good!

Bonnie: But then he got thrown in jail for a crime he didn't commit.

George: That was bad.

Bonnie: Soon he was put in charge of all the other prisoners . . .

George: That was good!

Bonnie: But still, he was stuck in jail year after year.

George: That was bad.

Bonnie: His friend got out and said he'd help Joseph get released!

George: That was good!

Bonnie: But then he forgot all about Joseph and left him in jail for two whole years.

George: That was really bad.

Bonnie: Finally, he remembered Joseph!

George: That was good!

Bonnie: And after bringing him to the king, Joseph interpreted the king's dreams and was put in charge of the whole land of Egypt, but he was still far from home and missed his dad and stuff.

George: (Confused) That was good . . . and bad . . . and good and stuff.

Bonnie: So not only was there no food in Egypt,

George: There was no food in any of the countries nearby.

Bonnie: So Jacob, Joseph's dad, heard there was food—

George: —At McDonald's.

Bonnie: No, at the king's palace in Egypt. So Jacob sent his ten oldest sons to Egypt. And who do you suppose they had to talk to in order to get their food?

George: Ronald McDonald?

Bonnie: No! Joseph! The guy in charge of all the food! He was—

George: —The Burger King.

Bonnie: Ugh! The governor! Now he recognized his brothers, but didn't let on that he knew who they really were.

George: Instead, he accused them of being spies.

Bonnie: But they said, "No! We're innocent!"

George: "Are not."

Bonnie: "Are too."

George: "Are not."

Bonnie: "Are too."

George: "Nope! You're spies! I win!"

Bonnie: So, Joseph decided to keep one brother in prison.

George: And he let the rest go home and waited to see if they would bring back his younger brother, Benjamin—wait a minute. Why do you think he did that?

Bonnie: Well, maybe to test them, or to see if their hearts had changed since that day when they plotted to kill him all those years earlier. He probably wanted to see if they would come back for their brother.

George: Oh.

Bonnie: Now, before they left, Joseph had one of his servants put the money back in their bags. Then when they got home, their father thought it was a trick and wouldn't let Benjamin return with them.

George: But finally, they did return to Egypt with Benjamin, and even more money,

Bonnie: To pay for both loads of food.

George: Now, when Joseph saw his younger brother, Benjamin,

Final Forgiveness

Bonnie: He realized how much he'd missed him so he went off by himself and cried.

George: *(Crying loudly like a baby)* Waa! Waa!

Bonnie: Not like that.

George: Oh. *(Act like a little kid)* I want my mommy!

Bonnie: Not like a little kid. He cried like a man.

George: Oh. *(Flex muscles while crying)* WAA! WAA!

Bonnie: At last he returned and told his servants to bring on the food for a great big feast.

George: Wait, I don't get it. Why was he accusing them of being spies and then inviting them over for dinner?

Bonnie: Well, despite all the bad stuff they'd done to him, he loved them. But he still wasn't sure if he could trust them.

George: Finally, it was time for all of them to leave. This time, Joseph had his servant put their money and his own silver cup into their bags.

Bonnie: When they left, he had his workers go and catch up with them.

George: "Hey! Why are you guys following us? What do you want?"

Bonnie: "You took Joseph's silver cup!"

George: "No way, Jose! If you find any of his stuff here, you can put to death the guy whose backpack it's in. And the rest of us will be your slaves! So there. Naa-naa-na-boo-boo!"

Bonnie: "OK, but we'll only enslave the guy who has the stolen goods."

George: "Whatever you want. We didn't take his sippy cup."

Bonnie: "Silver cup."

George: "Whatever."

Bonnie: *(Narrating)* They began to search all the sacks and when they got to Benjamin's pack, there was the silver cup.

George: That guy is dead meat.

Bonnie: Again, they all offered to be Joseph's slaves.

George: But again the servant said no. Only the guy who stole the silver cup—

Bonnie: —Must be a slave. So then, they returned to Joseph's palace and Judah offered to take the place of Benjamin. When Joseph saw that, he told his helpers to leave the room, and he began crying loudly.

George: WAA! WAA!

Bonnie: Um, not that loudly.

George: *(Softer)* Waa! Waa!

Bonnie: Then he told his brothers who he really was.

George: "I'm Spiderman."

Bonnie: *(Look accusingly at George)*

George: Ronald McDonald?

Bonnie: He said he was Joseph—

George: —By day, and a crime-fighting superhero by night!

Bonnie: *(Put your hands on your hips, and look severely at George)*

George: Sorry. "I'm Joseph, your long lost brother, the guy you sold as a slave when I was a kid."

Bonnie: The brothers were in shock.

George: "Holy Toledo."

Bonnie: "It's OK!" said Joseph. "Come here! You planned evil but God worked it all out for good."

George: Huh? What? But how could it be good?

Bonnie: God is in control of all things. Despite the evil choices of Joseph's brothers, God made something good happen, something good for the whole country.

Final Forgiveness

George: Oh. Cool.

Bonnie: Then they all hugged and wept and kissed and had a great big tear-fest.

George: *(Stand there motionless)*

Bonnie: Aren't you going to cry and stuff?

George: Naw. It was funny before, but I don't want to overdo it.

Bonnie: Then Jacob, their father, joined them all in Egypt,

George: And they lived sometimes happily and sometimes not so happily ever after,

Bonnie: But they realized God can work good

George: Even out of something bad.

Together: The end.

(Bow. Fade out the stage lights. Exit.)

THE KAYAK KID (MOSES)

BASED ON:	Exodus 1, 2
BIG IDEA:	God protected Moses as a baby and provided the right upbringing for him to become the mighty deliverer God had chosen him to be.
BACKGROUND:	After Joseph and his family settled in Egypt, their descendants had children and grandchildren and they grew numerous and prosperous in the land. One day, a king who hadn't heard of Joseph became the ruler in Egypt. He was afraid of the Israelites and oppressed them. Yet, through it all, they continued to prosper.
	Finally, the king ordered that all the Israelite boys be killed at birth. God used this situation to bring a great deliverer to his people and return them to the land that he had promised to Abraham and his descendants.
CAST:	Bonnie—A slightly more serious storyteller trying to tell the story (girl or boy)
	George—Her friend, who occasionally gets things mixed up (boy or girl)
	Note: These names are used only for the purpose of clarity in the script. You may wish to use the actual names of the two storytellers as you present the story.
PROPS:	A baby doll in a basket
TOPICS:	Family relationships, God's sovereignty, purpose, suffering
DIRECTOR'S TIPS:	Be sure your storytellers know how to pronounce the name of Moses' mother, *Jochebed.* (It rhymes with rock-a-bed.)
	The storytellers could be either boys or girls. Both readers start onstage or enter together. Bring up the stage lights and then begin when the students are quiet.

Teacher: **Lights! . . . Camera! . . . Action!**

Bonnie: **After Joseph and his family moved to Egypt, their descendants had children.**

George: **And their children had children.**

Bonnie: **And their children's children had children.**

George: **And their children's children's children had children. And their—**

Bonnie: **OK, I think they get the point.**

George: **One day, a new king became the ruler of Egypt.**

Bonnie: **He hadn't heard of Joseph,**

George: **And he was afraid of the Hebrews so he made them slaves and was very mean to them.**

Bonnie: **"Err . . . I hate all these Hebrews. I'll tell my slave drivers to make 'em work even harder!"**

George: **But still, the Hebrews continued to grow stronger and have lots of babies.**

Bonnie: **So the king of the Egyptians ordered that all the baby boys—**

George: —Go to daycare.

Bonnie: No. Actually, he ordered that they all be killed.

George: Yikes.

Bonnie: But the nurses who took care of the little babies kept hiding them,

George: *(Pick up the baby doll and try to hide him under your shirt or in your armpit or something.)*

Bonnie: Then one day, a baby was born to a woman named Jochebed.

George: Rock-a-bed, mock-a-bed, sock-a-bed too. I'm gonna drop a bed on top of you.

Bonnie: You are very weird.

George: Yup. Then she hid him for three months.

Bonnie: Which is a long time to hide a baby.

George: *(Make the baby cry, then hush the baby several times)* Waa! Waa! Shh! Shh! . . . Waa! Waa! Shh! Shh!

Bonnie: Finally, she couldn't hide him any longer because he was crying too loudly.

George: *(Holding up the baby)* WAA! WAA!

Bonnie: So she made a little basket, put the baby in the basket, and laid the basket at the edge of the Nile River.

George: Because there was no room for them at the inn.

Bonnie: What?

George: Oops. Wrong story.

Bonnie: She laid the baby in the Nile River. You might say he was in denial . . .

George: In denial?

Bonnie: Yeah. De-Nile. Get it? He was in de Nile River. Denial.

George: Oh. That was a joke.

Bonnie: Never mind.

George: Was he wearing a little helmet and kayaking down the rapids? *(Pretend to paddle a kayak)*

Bonnie: No. He was in the basket but his mother knew that downstream the princess would be taking her bath in the river. She was the daughter of Pharaoh, the king of Egypt!

George: In the river?

Bonnie: Right.

George: She took a bath in the river?

Bonnie: Uh-huh.

George: Without any clothes on?!

Bonnie: That's right.

George: Eek.

Bonnie: And the princess saw the basket floating in the reeds.

George: And that little baby inside, kayaking down the river. *(Pretend to paddle a kayak again, or move the doll's arms as if it's paddling)*

Bonnie: And so she went over, grabbed the basket—

George: —And taught him how to do an Eskimo roll. *(Tip the baby and the basket upside down and then rightside up again)*

Bonnie: She picked him up, and said,

George: *(Throughout this section, use the baby doll as a prop)* "Kootchie, kootchie, koo!"

Bonnie: Right.

George: "Kootchie, kootchie . . . uh-oh."

Bonnie: Uh-oh what?

George: *(Hold your nose. Wave the air away from the baby's bottom.)*

Bonnie: Ew . . . That's disgusting. Look, the princess's heart melted when she saw the baby, and she said,

The Kayak Kid

George: "Somebody change this kid's diaper. Yowsa!"

Bonnie: She said, "He must be one of those Hebrew boys." And just then, the baby's sister, Miriam, stepped up,

George: For she'd been waiting and watching and hiding nearby.

Bonnie: Yes. And she said, "I know a lady who could take care of that baby for you."

George: "Does she change stinky diapers?"

Bonnie: "Yup."

George: "She's got the job."

Bonnie: So, the girl ran off and brought her mom back to the princess, who hired her to raise the baby.

George: Wait a minute! She hired his own mom to take care of him?!

Bonnie: Yup.

George: This seems like a few too many coincidences to me. First, you've got the baby in the basket. Then you've got the naked princess without any clothes on taking a bath in a river, and the baby's sister showing up, and then his own mom getting hired to raise him!

Bonnie: You got it. That's exactly what happened.

George: Aha. So, God was in control all along?

Bonnie: Yup. He provided a way for this baby to be born, protected, raised, and taken care of.

George: So the princess officially adopted him,

Bonnie: And named him Moses.

Bonnie: *(insert the name of the other storyteller)* _____, do you know what Moses means?

George: Yes, I do.

Bonnie: Are you sure?

George: Yes. Absolutely.

Bonnie: So what does the name "Moses" mean?

George: "Man, can this kid kayak!"

Bonnie: No, no, no, that's not it.

George: "Somebody change this kid, he stinks!"

Bonnie: No. The word "Moses" sounds just like a Hebrew phrase that means, "taken from the water." The princess named him Moses because she took him from the water.

George: Huh. So, I guess today you'd call him "Driftwood."

Bonnie: Maybe.

George: So his mother helped raise him and when he became old enough, he decided to live and work with God's people instead of the Egyptians at the palace.

Bonnie: Because being close to God was more important to him than being rich and lazy.

George: You know, *(insert the name of the other storyteller)* _____, that's a pretty amazing story.

Bonnie: It sure is.

George: And there's just one thing I still don't get.

Bonnie: What's that?

George: Who taught Moses how to kayak anyway? His sister, his mom, or the naked princess?

Bonnie: Why do I put up with this?

Together: The end.

(Exit. As George leaves, he pretends to paddle a kayak offstage.)

The Kayak Kid

FLAMING FOLIAGE AND MAJOR PLAGUES (THE PLAGUES)

BASED ON: Exodus 3–14

BIG IDEA: God delivered his people from slavery to freedom.

BACKGROUND: After Moses fled from Egypt and started a new life as a shepherd, God spoke to him through a miraculous encounter at the burning bush, calling Moses to be his chosen deliverer for setting his people free. Despite Moses' initial reluctance to fulfill God's calling, he finally obeyed God and became one of the greatest prophets of all time.

In the second part of this story, when the king of Egypt refused to let God's people go, God sent a series of disasters on the land, bringing glory to himself and freedom to his people.

CAST: Two storytellers, one who reads the parts, the other who performs the actions and leads the listeners in imitating them.

PROPS: None

TOPICS: Consequences, courage, freedom, God's power, listening, obedience, Passover, prophecy fulfillment, second chances

DIRECTOR'S TIPS: For these two storymime scripts, it might be helpful if the person doing the actions has some experience in mime, theater, or just likes acting goofy. The storytellers could be either boys or girls.

With this type of storytelling one person serves as the primary storyteller and the other person does the actions or shows the emotions of the characters and events in the story. The speaking storyteller pauses after every action verb to allow time for her partner to act out what's happening in the story. Suggested actions are included.

Invite the audience to imitate, or "mime," the actions after the silent storyteller has performed them. This is a great way to include audience participation and works especially well with five- to ten-year olds. When doing this, just remember to have your reader wait long enough for the children to perform each action before continuing to read the next section.

This story has two parts to it. You may wish to perform them on different days, or perhaps do the first one at the beginning of your class period and then have games, activities, music, or crafts before performing the second part of the story. It may take too long to do both stories in a row.

When telling these two stories, the storytellers will both start onstage or enter together. Bring up the stage lights and then begin when the students are quiet.

Flaming Foliage and Major Plagues

STORYTELLER 1	STORYTELLER 2
PART 1—THE BURNING BUSH	
God protected Moses even when he was a baby.	*Stick your thumb in your mouth and make baby sounds.*
He grew taller . . .	*Put your hand about waist high.*
And taller . . .	*Raise your hand up to head height.*
And taller . . .	*Reach way up high.*
Until he was a man.	*Flex your muscles.*
One day he saw a guard beating up one of the Hebrews.	*Two fists up. Make a mean face.*
Moses was so angry, he attacked the guard.	*Hold up your hands in a karate stance. Make karate guy sounds.*
And the guard died.	*Slide your finger across your throat and stick out your tongue.*
And when the guard died, Moses hid the body in the sand.	*Grab a shovel and dig in the sand. Push a body in it.*
When everyone else found out, Moses ran away to another country.	*Run in place.*
He got a job watching over sheep.	*Put your hand above your eyes and scan the horizon.*
One day when he was on a mountain, he saw a burning bush that was not consumed.	*Hold hands out and warm them as if next to a campfire.*
God spoke through the fire and told Moses to take off his sandals.	*Reach down and pretend to take off your shoes. Then wave your hand in front of your nose as if your foot stinks.*
God told him, "Go to Egypt!"	*Point off into the distance.*
And Moses was like, "Who, me?"	*Point timidly to your chest.*
Because Moses was scared.	*Bite your fingernails and shake your knees.*
Then God told Moses, "Throw down your shepherd's staff.	*Pretend to throw a large stick onto the ground.*
See? It turned into a snake!	*Look surprised and scared.*
Pick it up!	*Point timidly to your chest again.*

Flaming Foliage and Major Plagues

Yes! Pick it up!"	*Pretend to pick up a snake that turns back into a stick.*
Then God told Moses, "Put your hand into your shirt.	*Slide your hand beneath your shirt.*
Now, pull it out."	*Pull it out and look shocked and surprised.*
Moses' hand was covered with a disease!	*Look terrified.*
And then God told him to put it back under his shirt.	*Nervously put your hand back in your shirt.*
And when he pulled his hand out this time, the disease was gone!	*Pull out your hand. You're healed! Huge smiles!*
Then God told Moses, "I will do these miracles.	*Point to your chest.*
Now go and set my people free!"	*Point off into the distance.*
Finally, Moses agreed to go back to Egypt.	*Put out your hands palms up and shrug your shoulders.*
He put on his sandals . . .	*Reach down and pretend to put your shoes on, then wave your hand in front of your nose as if your foot stinks.*
And went back to Egypt as God had commanded.	*Walk in place.*
The end.	*Take a bow.*

PART 2—THE PLAGUES

Moses met with the king of Egypt and told him to let God's people go. But the king said "no."	*Fold your arms and shake your head "no."*
God turned water into blood,	*Drink some. Spit it out.*
Sent about a million frogs,	*Stick out your tongue and pretend you're a frog catching a fly.*
Swarms of gnats to annoy the people,	*Wave your hands over your head like you're batting gnats away from your face.*
Like a billion flies,	*Run around buzzing.*
Sick cows,	*Act like you're going to throw up.*
Gross sores on the people,	*Make a nasty face and wipe your arm against someone else.*

Flaming Foliage and Major Plagues

The world's biggest hailstorm	*Put your hands over your head to protect yourself from the hail. One lands on your head. Ouch!*
Hordes of grasshoppers,	*Hop like a giant grasshopper.*
A deep and terrible darkness,	*Close your eyes and pretend to be a mime feeling his way across a wall.*
And still the king would not let God's people go.	*Fold your arms and shake your head "no."*
So finally, God let the firstborn Egyptians die and the king told the Israelites to go.	*You're sad. Cover your eyes with one hand and with the other point off into the distance.*
So the Israelites left the land and went into the desert.	*Walk in place. Wipe your brow as if you're sweaty.*
God led them with a tall towering cloud during the day . . .	*Stand up tall like a huge cloud. Wander around.*
And a tall towering wall of fire at night.	*Warm your hands against the sky.*
But when they got hungry, the Israelites grumbled against God.	*Fold your arms and look upset. Grumble.*
Then, the Egyptian army chased them and they were terrified!	*Shake, shiver, and bite your fingernails.*
But Moses raised his hand over the Red Sea.	*Lift one hand toward the sky.*
And the Lord sent a strong wind . . .	*Blow in your neighbor's face.*
That parted the waters.	*Swoop your hands out.*
So the Hebrews walked through the sea,	*Walk in place.*
With a wall of water on each side of them.	*Be a mime. Feel the walls beside you.*
But the Egyptians were angry.	*Look fierce and very angry.*
They rode their chariots fast after the Israelites.	*Pretend to ride a horse very fast.*
The walls of water washed over the Egyptians.	*Swoop your hands down in front of you.*
The Israelites were safe!	*Huge smiles.*
And they thanked God by doing a special dance.	*Dance around.*
The end.	*Take a bow.*

GOD'S SPY GUY (JOSHUA)

BASED ON: Numbers 13, 14; Deuteronomy 31:1-8; Joshua 1

BIG IDEA: Joshua was a brave warrior and spy. Even when God's people were ready to kill him, he continued to trust in God. After Moses died, Joshua became the leader of the children of Israel.

BACKGROUND: Aaron and Moses had been used by God to lead the Israelites out of slavery. When the Israelites arrived at the border of the Promised Land, Moses sent twelve spies to scout out the land. Ten of those spies doubted that God would give them victory in the land and convinced the Israelites that it would be better not to enter the land. Only Caleb and Joshua gave a good report and encouraged the people to trust in God and take over the land.

In the end, God forgave the Israelites, but the consequence for their doubt would be dying in the desert. In this script, Joshua recalls serving as a spy, and prepares to lead God's people into the Promised Land.

CAST: Bonnie—A slightly more serious storyteller trying to tell the story (girl or boy)
George—Her friend, who occasionally gets things mixed up (boy or girl)

Note: These names are used only for the purpose of clarity in the script. You may wish to use the actual names of the two storytellers as you present the story.

PROPS: None

TOPICS: Courage, God's power, obedience, planning, second chances

DIRECTOR'S TIPS: Both readers begin onstage or enter together. Bring up the stage lights and then begin when the students are quiet.

Teacher: **Lights! . . . Camera! . . . Action!**

Bonnie: **Long ago, God's people left Egypt,**

George: **And traveled through the desert.**

Bonnie: **They were tired,**

George: **And hot,**

Bonnie: **And sweaty,**

George: **And a little bit stinky.**

Bonnie: **But at last they came to the land God had promised to give them.**

George: **Moses gathered twelve men together to spy on the land.**

Bonnie: **"All right, men. I have a very important mission for you. I want you to sneak across the river. See if the land is good for crops and if the cities are strong. Be careful! And may God be with you."** *(Remain facing the audience)*

George: **So they crossed the river and spent the next forty days spying on the land.**

Bonnie: **The land was impressive.**

George: **"Dude, look at the impressive land."**

Bonnie: And the soil was great for growing things.

George: "Cool."

Bonnie: But the people of that land were huge and frightening.

George: "Oh. Bummer."

Bonnie: Two of the spies weren't scared, though. They trusted in God to be their leader.

George: "Right on, dude."

Bonnie: But the other ten spies were pretty much freaked out.

George: (Staring up at a giant) "Whoa, Mama. We're dead meat."

Bonnie: Finally, the spies returned.

George: And one of the ten frightened spies spoke up:

Bonnie: "We did what you told us, Moses! The soil is good. The grapes are great. But the people are huge! If we go in there, we'll be dead meat!"

George: But Caleb, one of the trusting spies, just said, "Let's go, dudes! God's on our side. We can so totally take these guys!"

Bonnie: But the other spies convinced God's people that they wouldn't be able to win—

George: —Even with God on their side.

Bonnie: And from then on, things went downhill fast.

George: All the Israelites started freaking out.

Bonnie: "Why did you ever take us out of Egypt, Moses? Now we're gonna die out here! Forget you! We need a new leader and we're going back to Egypt!"

George: So Moses and Aaron prayed to the Lord,

Bonnie: And Caleb and Joshua, the two good spies, ripped their clothes to show how sad they were.

George: Um, ripped their clothes?

Bonnie: Yes.

George: They ripped up their clothes?

Bonnie: Not all of their clothes.

George: Just the ones they were wearing?

Bonnie: Yes.

George: Could you see their bellybuttons?

Bonnie: Stop that.

George: Could you see their underwear?

Bonnie: I don't know. Let's get just back to the story.

George: OK. Whatever you say.

Bonnie: So, Caleb and Joshua were sad because the people wouldn't trust God—

George: —And because everyone could see their underwear.

Bonnie: Joshua and Caleb told the people that the Lord was with them and that they didn't need to be afraid,

George: But the people didn't listen and then they decided to kill Caleb and Joshua!

Bonnie: And then it happened. God's glory appeared to everyone.

George: (As an Israelite) "Uh-oh."

Bonnie: Moses told them that God would forgive everyone, but because of their rebellion, all the complainers wouldn't be allowed in the land.

George: (As an Israelite) "This is definitely not good."

Bonnie: But the people still didn't get it.

George: They were like, "OK, well I guess we better go into the land after all. We can take these guys! They're dead meat!"

God's Spy Guy

Bonnie: But it was too late. Moses told them they would fail because God wasn't gonna fight for them now. But they went anyway.

George: "Naw, we don't need God! Come on, everyone! Let's go conquer the land!"

Bonnie: And, just like Moses said, they got clobbered.

George: "Oops."

Bonnie: They lost the battle and a lot of people were killed . . .

George: "Ouch . . . Dead meat."

Bonnie: So, forty years went by.

George: And God's people spent the whole time wandering around in the desert.

Bonnie: They were more tired than before.

George: And hotter.

Bonnie: And sweatier

George: And a whole lot stinkier.

Bonnie: Until finally they arrived at the border of the Promised Land once again.

George: But Caleb and Joshua were the only two men left alive after those forty years.

Bonnie: Even Moses died.

George: Then God told Joshua that he had chosen him as the new leader.

Bonnie: And God told him,

George: "Be strong and courageous. Don't be afraid. I'll be with you. I'll never leave you alone."

Bonnie: And then Joshua sent a couple new spies into the land.

George: But he'd already decided to lead God's people into that land,

Bonnie: No matter what the spies said.

George: Finally, the people believed and followed the Lord,

Bonnie: And received all that God had promised them.

Together: The end.

(Bow. Fade out the stage lights. Exit.)

God's Spy Guy

THE DARING OUTCAST
(RAHAB)

BASED ON: Joshua 2; Hebrews 11:31; James 2:24, 25

BIG IDEA: Rahab welcomed the Jewish spies and protected them, even though it endangered her own life. She's a great example of faith in action.

BACKGROUND: After forty years of wandering in the desert, Joshua was ready to lead God's people into the Promised Land. Before crossing the Jordan River, he sent two spies into the land to bring back strategic information about the city of Jericho. Once inside the city, they stayed with a prostitute named Rahab. She'd placed her faith in the one true God (Hebrews 11:31), and the Lord was pleased with her when she put her faith into action (James 2:24, 25) by protecting the Israelite spies.

CAST: Rahab—An ex-prostitute who believed in the God of Israel and protected two Israelite spies when they came to her hometown of Jericho (girl)
Ditzy Airhead—An airhead TV talk show host (girl)

PROPS: Two chairs, an end table, two hand-held microphones (if desired)

TOPICS: Choices, conversion, courage, obedience

DIRECTOR'S TIPS: Ditzy Airhead's character is a true airhead, so have fun and ham it up. Consider having her wear a glitzy, ritzy, ditzy wig. Make sure that when she says the "La-La!" line that she does so in a sing-songy voice. Before starting the story, check to see if your reader can do this in an "airheady" way. If not, make up another saying that she can repeat throughout the drama.

    Both readers begin onstage, seated in the armchairs next to the end table. The stage should look like the set of a TV talk show. Bring up the stage lights and then begin when the students are quiet.

Teacher: **Lights! . . . Camera! . . . Action!**

Ditzy: **Ditzy Airhead, here.**

Rahab: **You're ditzy?**

Ditzy: **Uh-huh.**

Rahab: **And an airhead?**

Ditzy: **Right. I'm Ditzy Airhead.**

Rahab: **You're a ditzy airhead?**

Ditzy: **I'm the Ditzy Airhead.**

Rahab: *(To herself)* **Oh great.**

Ditzy: **Thank you.** *(To the audience)* **And we're here on our weekly TV show, "Women Who've Turned Their Lives Around."** *(In a sing-songy voice)* **La-La! And today's guest is a woman named Rahab. Thanks for joining us, Rahab.**

Rahab: Thanks, Ditzy. It's good to be here.

Ditzy: So, I understand you've had quite an adventure.

Rahab: Well, yes I have.

Ditzy: So tell us your story. Our viewers want to know all the juicy little details!

Rahab: Well, I used to have a job that wasn't very nice.

Ditzy: What was that? A talk show host? Oh, I'm just kidding. *(In a sing-songy voice)* La-La!

Rahab: Well, I'd go on dates with lots of different men.

Ditzy: Uh-huh.

Rahab: Who I wasn't married to.

Ditzy: Uh-huh.

Rahab: Because they were married to someone else.

Ditzy: Oh-ho . . .

Rahab: Yeah.

Ditzy: I see.

Rahab: So anyway, I know it didn't make God happy, but back then, that's what I did.

Ditzy: So, what happened to change your mind? Our viewers want to know!

Rahab: Well, I used to live in the city of Jericho.

Ditzy: Cherry Coke? You lived in a bottle of Cherry Coke? How refreshing!

Rahab: Not Cherry Coke, Ditzy, Jericho. It was a city with huge walls all around it to protect us from our enemies. And I lived in the city wall.

Ditzy: Oh. I thought so.

Rahab: You thought so, what?

Ditzy: *(Smiling and hinting)* I think you know.

Rahab: You think I know what?

Ditzy: I think you know what I thought you knew when I said I thought so!

Rahab: You mean, you thought I knew what you think I know that you thought, when you thought I knew you said so?

Ditzy: *(Confused)* I thought so.

Rahab: Oh. I don't even know what you're talking about any more.

Ditzy: The walls. The city. Enemies. Ooh.

Rahab: Right. Well, one day some soldiers came along.

Ditzy: Oh. Were they tall, dark, and handsome? La-La!

Rahab: I don't remember.

Ditzy: Oh.

Rahab: But I do remember they were looking for two spies.

Ditzy: Oh! Were the spies tall, dark, and handsome?

Rahab: Um. Not really.

Ditzy: Too bad . . . But, wait. You hid the spies, didn't you?

Rahab: Yup, under some stacks of stalks of flax.

Ditzy: Flax? What's flax?

Rahab: Flax is a plant stem that you can spin into thread.

Ditzy: Oh. There were stacks of flax?

Rahab: Right.

Ditzy: Stalks of flax.

Rahab: Yes.

Ditzy: Not sacks of flax?

Rahab: No.

Ditzy: Or racks of flax?

Rahab: No—

Ditzy: —Or flax in packs on the backs of yaks?

Rahab: What are you talking about?

Ditzy: I don't know. La-La!

Rahab: Oh.

Ditzy: So, tell us, what did you do? Were you scared? Ooh. It's so exciting. And dangerous. And romantic.

Rahab: Well, I wasn't really scared of them. I was more scared of the God of Israel than the—

Ditzy: —Stacks of flax?

Rahab: No, than the soldiers of Jericho.

Ditzy: So, lemme guess. The spies kidnapped you?

Rahab: No.

Ditzy: Attacked you and you had to use your black belt in karate to fend them off?

Rahab: I don't have a black belt in karate but I do have a scarlet thread.

Ditzy: In karate?

Rahab: No, in flax.

Ditzy: Oh, no. Not that again.

Rahab: I used the scarlet thread to hang out the window so that they could tell where I lived.

Ditzy: So they could come back over for pizza and a movie?

Rahab: No, so they wouldn't kill me and my family when they attacked and destroyed our town.

Ditzy: That was my second guess.

Rahab: So anyway, I helped them escape.

Ditzy: Why would you do that?

Rahab: Because I knew their God was going to destroy our city. And I'd learned their God is the Lord.

Ditzy: You're right. So, then what happened?

Rahab: Well, I let them hide under those stacks of stalks of flax—

Ditzy: —Stacks of stalks of flax?

Rahab: Right. And I told the soldiers here in Jericho that the spies had visited me and then run away.

Ditzy: So, you protected God's people?

Rahab: Yup, and they protected me. They didn't hurt my family when they attacked our town.

Ditzy: (To the audience) Well, folks, there you have it. Rahab protected the spies from prying eyes hidden in stacks of stalks of flax.

Rahab: Right.

Ditzy: Tune in next time for more of "Women Who've Turned Their Lives Around."

Rahab: Um, one thing, Ditzy. I didn't turn my life around, God did.

Ditzy: Did you get dizzy? La-La!

Rahab: You are a ditzy airhead.

Ditzy: Thank you!

Together: The end.

(Bow. Fade out the stage lights. Exit.)

THE WOMAN WARRIOR
(DEBORAH)

BASED ON: Judges 4, 5

BIG IDEA: Deborah exhibited courage and bravery by leading God's people into battle, even though at that time in history women weren't commonly military leaders.

BACKGROUND: The Israelites were stuck in a cycle of rebellion, regret, and repentance. Each time they turned to God, he raised up a leader from among them. One of those leaders was a woman named Deborah. She's the only woman judge (meaning a ruler, not a courtroom judge) listed in the book of Judges. Deborah was a prophetess, a political leader, a military strategist, and a songwriter. She used all of her gifts to serve and honor God.

CAST: Bonnie—A slightly more serious storyteller trying to tell the story (girl or boy)
George—Her friend, who occasionally gets things mixed up (boy or girl)

Note: These names are used only for the purpose of clarity in the script. You may wish to use the actual names of the two storytellers as you present the story.

PROPS: None

TOPICS: Courage, faithfulness, giftedness, leadership, purpose, success

DIRECTOR'S TIPS: During parts of this story, George sings his own version of lines from the song "On Top of Old Smokey." Make sure he's familiar with these phrases and with the tune before beginning the story.

This script contains a number of unusual names, so before presenting the story, make sure your readers know how to pronounce all the words.

The storytellers could be either boys or girls. Both readers start onstage or enter together. Bring up the stage lights and then begin when the students are quiet.

Teacher: Lights! . . . Camera! . . . Action!

Bonnie: OK, to understand today's story, you have to understand who the good guys are and who the bad guys are.

George: I already know who the good guys are.

Bonnie: Who?

George: Michael Jordan, Tiger Woods, Tony Hawk—*(or other popular athletes or movie stars)*

Bonnie: —None of those guys are in this story.

George: Why not?

Bonnie: This story takes place a long time ago.

George: Oh. Tarzan. Robin Hood—

Bonnie: —Listen, in this story the good guys are the Israelites and the bad guys are the Canaanites.

George: Did you just say, "Stain your tights?"

Bonnie:	No. Canaanites!
George:	Oh. Got it. That's a lot better than staining your tights.
Bonnie:	Yes it is. And the leader of the Canaanite's army was a man named Sisera.
George:	Sounds like Sahara.
Bonnie:	No, he wasn't a desert; he was a guy who led the army and he had 900 iron chariots and attacked the Israelites for twenty years. Now, the leader of the Israelites was a woman named Deborah. She was a prophetess and a leader of the people.
George:	Wow. She sounds cool.
Bonnie:	She was cool.
George:	Girl power.
Bonnie:	You got it. And then the Israelites asked God for help so that they could beat Mr.—
George:	—Sizzling hair.
Bonnie:	Sisera.
George:	Right.
Bonnie:	Well, Deborah called in her own army commander, a guy named Barak. And she told him to take 10,000 men up the mountain to fight Sisera.
George:	And Barak was like, "Um, that sounds dangerous."
Bonnie:	"It is."
George:	"Well, if you come with me, I'll go. But if you don't come with me, I'm not going anywhere."
Bonnie:	And Deborah just shook her head. "What a baby! OK, but if I come you're not gonna get any credit for winning this fight. Instead, the honor will go to a woman."
George:	"Okey-dokey. Girl power."
Bonnie:	You got it. So then Barak gathered 10,000 men.

George:	Wait, let me get this straight. There were 10,000 men and one woman leading them?
Bonnie:	Yup.
George:	Mega-girl power.
Bonnie:	Actually, it was more than just girl power. It was God power.
George:	Gotcha.
Bonnie:	Then Sisera heard they were coming, so he got his army ready.
George:	Oh, yes. We're getting to the good part.
Bonnie:	God fought on the side of the Israelites—
George:	—The good guys.
Bonnie:	And helped them totally destroy the Canaanites—
George:	—The bad guys with stained tights.
Bonnie:	Sisera saw he was losing, so he ran away and looked for a place to hide. At last he found a tent owned by this lady named Jael.
George:	So . . . he went to jail.
Bonnie:	Well, yeah. And then he asked her for a drink and she gave him some milk and he fell asleep.
George:	Oh, yeah, yeah. I know this part. It's really awesome.
Bonnie:	And she took a long tent stake and—
George:	—Lemme do this part.
Bonnie:	Um . . . I shouldn't do this, but OK. Go ahead.
George:	Deborah wrote a song about it, right?
Bonnie:	Well, yes.
George:	So, I wrote a song about it too.
Bonnie:	Oh, no. Go ahead.

George: *(Singing to the tune of "On Top of Old Smokey")* "Inside of her tent ol' Sisera had fled—"

Bonnie: —OK, very nice—

George: *(Continuing the song)* —"But Jael took a tent peg,"

Bonnie: Uh-huh.

George: *(Singing)* "And slammed it right through his head."

Bonnie: Gross.

George: *(Singing)* "It went through his brains and they oozed on the floor—"

Bonnie: —All right! That's enough!

George: *(Singing)* "And Sisera didn't ride his iron chariot no more."

Bonnie: Will you stop that? Why did you have to make your song so gross?

George: Well, Deborah did too. Didn't she? She wrote a song just about like it.

Bonnie: Yeah, I guess you're right.

George: She was cool!

Bonnie: Right. And she wanted everyone to know that God was more powerful than any of the enemies of the land.

George: It must have worked too, because there was peace in the land for the next forty years.

Bonnie: Right.

George: And she was right about a woman getting all the credit.

Bonnie: Right.

George: So, the good guys won.

Bonnie: Yup.

George: And the bad guys lost.

Bonnie: Uh-huh.

George: And Sisera's brains oozed out all over the floor.

Bonnie: You are disgusting, you know that?

George: Why, thank you.

Together: The end.

(Bow. Fade out the stage lights. Exit.)

The Woman Warrior

THE UNLIKELY HERO

(GIDEON)

BASED ON: Judges 6, 7

BIG IDEA: Even though Gideon wasn't experienced as a leader, God chose him and gifted him for a specific purpose. God gifts us to serve him too.

BACKGROUND: For seven years the Midianites had been oppressing the Israelites. They destroyed the Israelite flocks, herds, and crops. Finally, when the Israelites called out to the Lord, the Angel of the Lord appeared to timid Gideon and gave him the job of leading God's people to freedom.

CAST: Bonnie—A slightly more serious storyteller trying to tell the story (girl or boy)
George—Her friend, who occasionally gets things mixed up (boy or girl)

Note: These names are used only for the purpose of clarity in the script. You may wish to use the actual names of the two storytellers as you present the story.

PROPS: A container of wheat germ; if possible, a baseball cap from the Angels baseball team

TOPICS: Angels, courage, following God, freedom, God's power, Holy Spirit, purpose, resentment, success

DIRECTOR'S TIPS: The readers could be either boys or girls. Both readers start onstage or enter together. Bring up the stage lights and then begin when the students are quiet.

Teacher: **Lights! . . . Camera! . . . Action!**

Bonnie: **Once upon a time there was this guy named Gideon.**

George: **That's me!**

Bonnie: **One day he was throwing up wheat—**

George: **—What?!**

Bonnie: **Throwing up wheat . . .**

George: **That's disgusting.**

Bonnie: **No, he was throwing it up high into the air.**

George: **That's even worse.**

Bonnie: **Listen, he was taking handfuls of wheat and tossing them into the air so the wind would separate the wheat from the chaff.**

George: **Oh. I thought you meant—**

Bonnie: **—I know what you thought. But he was tossing the wheat into the air to make cereal.**

George: *(Toss wheat germ into the air)* **Yummy. I'm making cereal by throwing wheat in the air. How cool is that?**

Bonnie:	When an angel of the Lord appeared before him. *(Put a baseball cap on, then turn and face your storytelling partner)*
George:	Ah! Who are you?
Bonnie:	"I am the Angel of the Lord!"
George:	Why are you wearing a baseball cap?
Bonnie:	"I'm a big fan of the angels. Get it? The baseball team?"
George:	Was that supposed to be funny?
Bonnie:	"I guess not . . . I am with you, mighty warrior!"
George:	Do I look like a mighty warrior to you?
Bonnie:	"You are Gideon, the mighty warrior!"
George:	I think you got the wrong guy, buddy. I'm not a mighty warrior. I'm a wimpy warrior. No, wait. I'm not even a warrior. *(Looking at the wheat)* Cereal Man maybe, but Mighty Warrior—um, that would be a "no." I'm just the grain guy.
Bonnie:	*(Taking off your hat, you're no longer the angel. Speak to the audience)* And then, Gideon got mad.
George:	Wait a minute, Mr. Angel-of-the-Lord. If God's really with us, how come our enemies, the Midianites, are always attacking us? Huh? Huh? Huh? Where are all the miracles we hear about all the time? Nope, God isn't with us anymore. I don't believe you.
Bonnie:	And then, Gideon returned to his work.
George:	*(Toss more wheat germ into the air)* Throwing up my wheat.
Bonnie:	But the Lord told him, "I am sending you." And then Gideon realized it wasn't just any old angel that was there, it was really the not-yet-born Savior of the world—
George:	—Jesus—
Bonnie:	—Right. And the Lord said, "Go in the strength I've given you. Save your land."

George:	*(To Bonnie)* Wait a minute. You mean to tell me that it was really God?
Bonnie:	Yup.
George:	And Gideon told him off?
Bonnie:	Yup.
George:	And God didn't get mad?
Bonnie:	Nope.
George:	Why not?
Bonnie:	God was patient with Gideon, even when Gideon doubted him. And then Gideon said,
George:	"How am I supposed to do all that? I'm telling you, I'm not a mighty warrior! See?" *(Throw some more wheat germ into the air)*
Bonnie:	But the Lord told him, "I'll be with you. Go on. You'll clobber those guys."
George:	With what? Shredded wheat? Look, could you give me a sign?
Bonnie:	*(As God)* "Sure."
George:	Great.
Bonnie:	So, Gideon went and roasted a goat.
George:	That was his sign?
Bonnie:	Just roast the goat; you'll see what I mean.
George:	*(Stick an imaginary goat in the oven)* Yummy.
Bonnie:	Then God said, "Put it on the rock over there."
George:	*(Put the imaginary food on the imaginary rock)* OK, now what?
Bonnie:	"Step back."
George:	*(Step back)*
Bonnie:	Then the Angel of the Lord made fire burn it all up, and Gideon said,

The Unlikely Hero

George: Holy Toledo. That's one hot rock.

Bonnie: No, he said,

George: If you were hungry why didn't you just say so?

Bonnie: Listen. He said, "Ah! I've seen God face to face!"

George: Ah! I've seen God face to face!

Bonnie: "I'm a goner for sure!"

George: I'm a goner for sure!

Bonnie: But God told him, "Don't worry, I came to help you, not kill you. And you will be a mighty warrior called—"

George: —Cereal Man!

Bonnie: Then, God gave him more signs.

George: And finally,

Bonnie: After God's Spirit came to help him, he was ready to go,

George: I was ready to go.

Bonnie: He gathered up 32,000 men.

George: I gathered up 32,000 men.

Bonnie: And then God said, "Not so fast."

George: And then I said . . . wait a minute! What did you just say?

Bonnie: God told Gideon, "Not so fast. That's too many men. Anyone who's scared can go home."

George: I'll bet none of them left.

Bonnie: 22,000 men left.

George: Oh. Well I was close.

Bonnie: But God still wasn't done. God kept trimming the number until there were only 300 men left.

George: Um. How am I supposed to win a war with only 300 men?

Bonnie: You're not.

George: I'm not?

Bonnie: Nope. God is.

George: Oh. Yeah. Right. I get it.

Bonnie: And God was going to do it all through Gideon!

George: Are you kid-eon?

Bonnie: As he fought against Midian

George: Even though he felt like quit-eon.

Bonnie: Would you stop all the rhyming already?

George: Wanna go to the prime meridian?

Bonnie: (Sigh) So, after God cut the size of his army down the men grabbed some—

George: —Machine guns and photon lasers. Now, that's what I'm talking about!

Bonnie: No, water jars and trumpets.

George: They went to war with a bunch of canteens?

Bonnie: Well, clay pots.

George: That's it?

Bonnie: Yes. And trumpets. And Gideon ordered the men,

George: Follow my lead! When I blow my trumpet, you blow yours and . . . we'll blow those Midianites away!

Bonnie: Right. So, they snuck over to the Midian camp. They broke their jars and blew their trumpets. And yelled,

George: A sword for the Lord and for Gideon!

Bonnie: Then, the Midianites got confused—

George: —And started playing their tubas.

The Unlikely Hero

Bonnie: No. Uh-uh.

George: Harmonicas?

Bonnie: No, they started killing each other. And finally, when it was all done, God's people were the winners.

George: Cool. Good for us!

Bonnie: And then the people wanted to make Gideon their king!

George: King Cereal Man!

Bonnie: Um. He didn't let them.

George: Oh.

Bonnie: Instead, he said, "I won't be your king. God will!"

George: I won't be your king. God will!

Bonnie: And the people chose to serve God, and finally there was peace in the land.

Together: The end.

(Bow. Fade out the stage lights. Exit.)

THE REAL-LIFE SUPERHERO
(SAMSON)

BASED ON: Judges 13–16; Hebrews 11:32

BIG IDEA: Samson kept taking revenge on the people who wronged him; however, God still used him in a mighty way to fight the enemies of the Israelites.

BACKGROUND: During the time of the judges, God sent his Spirit on a man named Samson. God's Spirit gave Samson great power, not for preaching or teaching, but to fight as a mighty warrior. Even though Samson didn't always use wise judgment or honor God with his choices, God still used him to rescue his people. Samson is listed in Hebrews 11:32 as a man of great faith.

CAST: Narrator—a storyteller who tells the story of Samson's life (boy or girl)
Samson—a storyteller who tells the story from Samson's perspective (boy)

PROPS: None, or you may wish to have Samson wear a wig

TOPICS: Courage, following God, giftedness, leadership, second chances, success, vengeance

DIRECTOR'S TIPS: Note that sometimes Samson will do the actions that the Narrator describes. Let Samson look over the script beforehand to make sure he's familiar with the actions.
  Both readers begin onstage or enter together. Bring up the stage lights and then begin when the students are quiet.

Teacher: **Lights! . . . Camera! . . . Action!**

Narrator: **Once upon a time, long ago, God gave great strength to a man named Samson.**

Samson: *(Flex your muscles)*

Narrator: **God's Spirit gave Samson strength because of his long hair. In fact, he had never had a haircut in his whole life.**

Samson: *(Poof your hair)*

Narrator: **Samson was so strong that one day he fought off 1,000 Philistine soldiers—they were the bad guys—with the jawbone of a donkey as his only weapon.**

Samson: *(Fight off the Philistines. Add sound effects. Go wild.)*

Narrator: **He was so thirsty he thought he was going to die.**

Samson: *(Act tired and thirsty)* **I think I'm gonna die.**

Narrator: **But he didn't die.**

Samson: **That's a good thing.**

Narrator: **God had another plan. God sent Samson to find a girlfriend from another country.**

Samson: **Yowsa. Man, was she cute.**

Narrator: On his way to see her, Samson met a lion. It roared toward him and leaped into the air trying to eat him alive.

Samson: *(Act out these things as you say them)* **Poor little kitty. I just grabbed it like this . . . and pulled it apart like this . . . and ripped it open like this . . . and yanked its insides out.**

Narrator: Yuck.

Samson: Cool.

Narrator: The wedding didn't work out between Samson and that lady, but God did use it as a chance for Samson to fight against the bad guys once again.

Samson: *(Act out a fight scene)* **Take that! . . . and that! . . . and a little of that! . . . hi-ya-ka-bung-ah!**

Narrator: Yup. Ol' Samson had lots of adventures and he was the mightiest warrior in all the land.

Samson: *(Flex muscles)*

Narrator: But he had one problem: no matter what happened, Samson always tried to get revenge on the people who hurt him.

Samson: I can't stand those Philistines. I'll do worse to them than they did to me!

Narrator: Then, Samson met another girl.

Samson: Yowsa.

Narrator: Her name was Delilah.

Samson: I like girls.

Narrator: And she was really cute.

Samson: Whoa, mama. Delightful Delilah.

Narrator: But when the Philistines discovered they were going out together, they convinced Delilah to find out the secret to Samson's great strength.

Samson: At first I made up all sorts of weird things. Tie me up . . . Make a quilt out of my hair . . . Just weird stuff like that.

Narrator: But then, she just kept nagging and nagging and nagging until he couldn't stand it anymore.

Samson: OK, OK! All right, already! It's all in the hair, baby. All in the hair!

Narrator: That night, while he was sleeping,

Samson: *(Snoring)*

Narrator: The bad guys snuck in.

Samson: *(Snoring)*

Narrator: And chopped off Samson's hair. *(If you're using a wig prop, pull it off Samson's head.)*

Samson: Uh-oh. Hair today, gone tomorrow.

Narrator: Then, they paid off their helper, Delilah, and took Samson away to jail.

Samson: Yikes. I'm as bald as a cue ball. *(Try to fight. You're a weakling now.)* **And as weak as a cue ball.**

Narrator: While he was in prison, three things began to happen. His hair began to grow . . . *(If you're using a wig prop, stick it back on Samson's head.)*

Samson: *(Poof your hair)*

Narrator: His heart began to change . . .

Samson: *(Pretend to pray)*

Narrator: And his strength began to return . . .

Samson: *(Flex your muscles)*

Narrator: One last time, Samson asked God to send him great strength. God answered his prayer.

Samson: *(REALLY flex your muscles)*

Narrator: And so, when the Philistines brought him out to make fun of him,

Samson: *(As the Narrator describes these events, Samson acts them out)*

The Real-life Superhero

Narrator: He grabbed the two posts holding up the building . . . And pushed them to the ground . . .

Samson: Hi-ya-ka-bung-ah!

Narrator: And smushed everyone there . . . including himself.

Samson: Um . . . Ouch?

Narrator: But the story of Samson lives on because he was one of God's heroes,

Samson: Even though he was a bald guy.

Narrator: Do you know the moral of the story?

Samson: Never trust your girlfriend with a pair of scissors when you fall asleep.

Narrator: No.

Samson: Bald men are weaker than hairy men?

Narrator: No. The moral is—use the gifts God gives you,

Samson: And don't waste 'em.

Narrator: And let God work through you,

Samson: To accomplish his plans.

Together: The end.

(Bow. Fade out the stage lights. Exit.)

The Real-life Superhero

The Dutiful Daughter-in-law (Ruth)

BASED ON: Ruth

BIG IDEA: Ruth faithfully trusted in God and honored her mother-in-law. She left her home and her own people and became one of the ancestors of Joseph, the husband of Mary, Jesus' mother.

BACKGROUND: Because of a drought, Naomi and her family moved from Bethlehem to the country of Moab. Once there, her sons got married. Sometime later, her husband and two sons died, leaving Naomi bitter and alone. One of her daughters-in-law, a kindhearted young lady named Ruth, returned to Bethlehem with Naomi. Through a series of divinely orchestrated events, Naomi saw how God continued to work through tragedy to bring about a future blessing for his followers. Ruth modeled great faith in the Lord and unhesitating devotion to her family.

CAST: Ruth—A young woman from Moab who has chosen to follow and believe in the God of the Israelites (girl)
Les Braincell—A corny, bumbling, overenthusiastic detective investigating a trespassing accusation (boy)

PROPS: A trench coat, notepad, magnifying glass for Les

TOPICS: Disappointment, faithfulness, family relationships, God's sovereignty, grief and loss, obedience, purpose

DIRECTOR'S TIPS: Les Braincell's character is meant to be corny, so choose a reader who can ham it up, be goofy, exaggerated, and silly. Since he appears in several skits, you may wish to use the same costume each time he makes an appearance. Les starts the scene onstage. Bring up the lights and then begin when the students are quiet.

Teacher: **Lights! . . . Camera! . . . Action!**

Les: **I'm Les, Les Braincell here, the world's greatest detective. On the scene here in Bethlehem . . .** *(Look through the magnifying glass as Ruth enters)* **where there was the report of a strange woman leaving the threshing floor.**

Ruth: **Hey, who are you calling strange?!**

Les: **So, you're the woman?**

Ruth: **I'm a woman.**

Les: **So, you admit it then!!!**

Ruth: **Admit what?**

Les: **It was you!**

Ruth: **What was me?**

Les: **Are you trying to deny it now? Weasel out of it? Maybe plead the fifth amendment?**

Ruth: What's the fifth amendment?

Les: I have no idea. But it sure sounds official.

Ruth: What are you talking about?

Les: Were you at the threshing floor?

Ruth: Yes, but I wasn't breaking any rules. Listen, it's kind of a long story.

Les: Has it been made into a movie yet? I always prefer the movie to the book.

Ruth: Boaz was a friend of mine and I went there to the threshing floor to . . . well . . . let him know I wanted to marry him.

Les: Aha!!!

Ruth: You see, my mother-in-law, Naomi, had it rough. Her husband and her two sons all died. We were both very sad, and then she became angry at God.

Les: Aha!!! So. It was all God's fault. I guess I'll have to take him in.

Ruth: It wasn't God's fault. It's not his fault we die, it's ours. Sin is the cause of death.

Les: You know the cause of death? Well, then I guess we've solved this case.

Ruth: You're not investigating a murder.

Les: I'm not? Then what am I doing here?

Ruth: Threshing floor, remember?

Les: Ah. Yes. So what was I doing there in the middle of the night?

Ruth: You weren't there, I was.

Les: Aha!!!

Ruth: Aha what? Why do you keep saying that?

Les: No reason. I just like saying "Aha!!!"

Ruth: Oh.

Les: So, what on earth is a threshing floor, anyway?

Ruth: It's a place where they clean the wheat and prepare it to be made into cereal.

Les: So . . . now there's a cereal killer on the loose too . . .

Ruth: Has anyone ever told you that you're very weird?

Les: Yes, they have. (*Looking her over closely with the magnifying glass*) Why do you think that is?

Ruth: Hmm. It's a mystery to me.

Les: Nothing's a mystery to me . . . Except why I don't laugh when I tickle myself. That's always bothered me . . .

Ruth: Anyway, after a while Naomi and I went back to Bethlehem.

Les: To see the baby Jesus?

Ruth: He isn't going to be born for like 800 years.

Les: Whew. That's a long time to be pregnant.

Ruth: Well, when I moved back here from Moab, I went to Boaz's fields to gather wheat.

Les: Did you pay for it?

Ruth: No.

Les: Stealing wheat! So you admit that too, huh?

Ruth: We're supposed to do it.

Les: You are?

Ruth: Yeah. Naomi and I didn't have any money or a job, so we couldn't get food. Boaz and his workers left lots of grain for me to take home. After that, Naomi encouraged me to meet with Boaz,

Les: On the threshing floor.

Ruth: Right. And pretty soon we were dating and then we got married; we had a baby boy, and our baby's, baby's, baby's, baby's baby—

The Dutiful Daughter-in-law

Les: —800 years from now,

Ruth: Yeah, will one day have a baby who is Joseph, the husband of Mary, the mother of Jesus.

Les: Who was born 2000 years ago in Bethlehem . . .

Ruth: It might be the past for you, but it's still the future for me.

Les: Right . . .

Ruth: And then, Naomi helped raise my baby. And she learned that God is faithful after all.

Les: So, I guess that about wraps up the case. I'm afraid I'm going to have to arrest you.

Ruth: But why?

Les: Well, for impersonating a Bible character, trespassing, stealing wheat, going to a threshing floor, and marrying a guy named Boaz!

Ruth: Oh. But I am a Bible character, I didn't steal or trespass or anything. It's not illegal to go to a threshing floor. And what's wrong with marrying a guy named Boaz?

Les: I don't know. I wouldn't do it.

Ruth: I would hope not.

Les: OK, you're free to go then. But what makes you a Bible hero, anyway?

Ruth: I wouldn't say I'm a hero.

Les: But you believed in God through everything.

Ruth: Yeah.

Les: And that makes you a hero of faith.

Ruth: I'm just glad God could use me; that's all.

Les: And I'm just glad I have this magnifying glass.

Ruth: You're very weird.

Les: Thank you, but flattery will get you nowhere.

Together: The end.

(Bow. Fade out the stage lights. Exit.)

THE GIANT MATCH-UP
(DAVID AND GOLIATH)

BASED ON: 1 Samuel 17

BIG IDEA: With God's help, David killed Goliath and became one of Israel's greatest heroes.

BACKGROUND: God's people, the Israelites, were embroiled in a conflict with the ruthless Philistines. Saul, the king of Israel, was beginning to show cowardice as a leader. When no one else stepped up to face Goliath, a young man with great faith in God came forward to fight the giant. As a result, the Israelites rallied and a new era of conquest began for God's people.

CAST: Bo and Gary are TV sports announcers giving the play-by-play of David's victory over Goliath. Bo is somewhat clueless yet a bit of a "know-it-all." Gary has more of the right answers.

PROPS: Papers, clipboards, microphones

TOPICS: Bullies, conviction, courage, faith, giftedness, God's power, success

DIRECTOR'S TIPS: Encourage your actors to have fun pretending to be sports announcers during this story. You may wish to have them dress the part with old suit coats and microphones. Whenever Bo says, "Thaaaaaaaaat's rrrrrrrrrrright, Gary, I do!" he does it very, very dramatically. Practice with your actors first.

The actors could be either boys or girls. Both actors start onstage or enter together. Bring up the stage lights and then begin when the students are quiet.

Teacher: **Lights! . . . Camera! . . . Action!**

Gary: *(To the audience)* **Gary Gumball with Bo Donut, reporting to you from Sports Central Live.**

Bo: **Well, Gary, we're here at the scene of the battle today. And, as you know, it promises to be a great fight!**

Gary: **It sure does, Bo. On one side we've got the Israelites, and on the other side the Philistines. And the Philistines' best athlete is a guy name Goliath. He measures in at over nine feet tall!**

Bo: **That's a big 'ole boy.**

Gary: **And he's looking for a fight, but no one seems to be stepping up to the plate to face the challenge.**

Bo: **Well, you know what they say, "The bigger they are, the harder they are to feed."**

Gary: **Um, I think you mean, "The bigger they are, the harder they fall."**

Bo: **Thaaaaaaaaat's rrrrrrrrrrright, Gary. I do!!! But wait! What's this? There's a kid running out onto the playing field! *(To audience)* Hey, kid! Come back here!**

Gary: Wait, Bo. That's not a lost boy. That's the guy from the Israelites' team who's gonna fight the giant.

Bo: Whew! In that case, it's kinda like David going up against Goliath out there today.

Gary: Bo, it is David going up against Goliath out there today.

Bo: Thaaaaaaaaat's rrrrrrrrrrright, Gary. It is!!! Well, let's see what happens. (Shuffling through papers) We don't have too many stats on this kid. He must have just moved up from the minors.

Gary: (Reading from a stat sheet) It says here, he was a shepherd.

Bo: I've never heard of that team before—

Gary: —It isn't a team, Bo. I mean, the boy watched over the sheep. And, he's a songwriter.

Bo: So he's more qualified to take care of the mascot or sing the national anthem than to face this giant . . .

Gary: Well, he once killed a lion and a bear with his bare hands . . .

Bo: And look at this! He came here today delivering cheese sandwiches! Hmm . . . I'm getting hungry . . . .

Gary: (Pause for a moment, look at Bo as if to say, "What are you talking about?" Then point in the distance) There he goes! He has a stick and a slingshot.

Bo: That's it? I don't believe it! That giant has an industrial strength Kevlar bulletproof vest! Reinforced airline steel shield! A spear as big as a missile—

Gary: Wait a minute . . . Listen . . . We've got audio from Goliath's headset microphone. (Cover your mouth and speak for Goliath) "Ha! What do I look like? A dog? You want me to fetch your sticks!"

Bo: He's talking trash, Gary.

Gary: He sure is, Bo.

Bo: Wait, I believe we're getting a live satellite feed from David's mike . . . (Cover your mouth and speak for David). "We don't need no stinking weapons! The Lord is on our side!" (Shuffle papers, look for info) Hm . . . The Lord . . . Let's see . . . I don't see him on the roster . . .

Gary: There goes the giant and his shield-holder. They're moving in fast!

Bo: And what's this? There goes the boy. He's running in toward the giant! I repeat, he's running in toward the giant!

Gary: You know, Bo, David's showing some good speed out there today.

Bo: He sure is, Gary.

Gary: He's reaching into his shepherd's bag. Nice form.

Bo: He's got a stone. He's putting it into his sling.

Gary: The giant is raising his spear.

Bo: David's swinging the stone over his head. I repeat, David is swinging the stone over his head!

Gary: The excitement is building.

Bo: Goliath doesn't seem fazed at all by this, Gary. He's still moving toward the kid.

Gary: The stone is released,

Bo: It's a fast ball,

Gary: We're clocking it at 107 miles per hour!

Bo: There's only a handful of people in the world who can sling a rock at speeds like that.

Gary: That kid from Bethlehem has got some arm.

Bo: Thaaaaaaaaat's rrrrrrrrrrright, Gary. He does!!!

Gary: And Goliath seems to think he can best deflect that stone by using his forehead.

The Giant Match-up

Bo: I would have used my shield in a situation like that, Gary.

Gary: Me, too, Bo. But let's see what happens. This giant's got lots of battle experience—

Bo: —Oh! The stone has sunk into the giant's forehead. I repeat, the stone has sunk into the giant's forehead!

Gary: It's lodged in there, oh, about five or six inches.

Bo: That's gotta hurt.

Gary: Yeah, he's gonna feel that one in the morning.

Bo: That's what I call using your head.

Gary: He's on his way down.

Bo: He's falling . . .

Gary: Falling . . .

Bo: Falling . . .

(Both actors bump up and down on their chairs as the giant hits the ground)

Gary: Yikes.

Bo: The giant has hit the ground.

Gary: And here comes David. He's running toward the giant.

Bo: What's he gonna do, Gary? Maybe a little end-zone dance?

Gary: I don't know, Bo . . . Nope, look at that. He's got the giant's sword in his hand.

Bo: Good game plan. He didn't bring his own sword so he's gonna use the giant's sword instead!

Gary: Brilliant strategy!

Bo: Oh, look at that. He's cutting off the head of the giant. I repeat, he's cutting off the head of the giant!

Gary: You know, Bo, any time you get your head cut off like that, it really takes the fight out of you.

Bo: It sure does, Gary.

Gary: And there go the Philistines.

Bo: Check out the look in their eyes!

Gary: Yup. Looks to me like they're either terrified or they've gotta go to the bathroom really bad.

Bo: So, the Philistines are taking off.

Gary: And here come the Israelites!

Bo: The race is on!

Gary: And it looks like—yes! Yes! The Philistines are getting kicked all over the field!

Bo: Yikes. It's not looking good for them here today. They're getting cut down left and right by the Israelites. I repeat, *(motion for the audience to join you as you say this)* they're getting cut down left and right by the Israelites!

Gary: It looks like David and the Lord were victorious out there today!

Bo: It sure does, Gary.

Gary: And it looks like David is gonna keep the giant's head as a souvenir.

Bo: Ew . . . I hope he's not going to mount it on the wall above his fireplace.

Gary: I don't think he will, Bo.

Bo: Why not?

Gary: His tent doesn't have a fireplace.

Bo: Thaaaaaaat's rrrrrrrrrright, Gary. It doesn't!!!

Gary: Well, that's our game for today! Join us next time for more live coverage!

Bo: Until then, this is Bo Donut,

Gary: And Gary Gumball, signing off!

Together: The end.

(Bow. Fade out the stage lights. Exit.)

The Giant Match-up

THE BARBECUE ON CARMEL MOUNTAIN (ELIJAH)

BASED ON: 1 Kings 17:1; 18:1-46

BIG IDEA: On Mt. Carmel, God proved that he was the one true God. Finally, the Israelites turned back to him.

BACKGROUND: Ahab and his family were wicked rulers in the northern kingdom of Israel. As a result, God's prophet Elijah prayed that God would not send rain or dew on the land. The Israelites were worshiping Baal, a god of fertility, but Elijah's simple prayer showed how worthless this "god" was. During the three-year drought, God protected and provided for Elijah in miraculous ways.

Finally, God told Elijah to set up a showdown where he would prove once and for all that he really was the Lord.

Elijah boldly stood up for the Lord in front of 450 prophets of Baal. God proved that he alone is for real. As a result, the Israelites turned their hearts to the Lord.

CAST: Two storytellers, one who reads the parts, the other who leads the actions.

PROPS: None

TOPICS: Choices and consequences, courage, faith, following God, God's existence, God's power, idolatry, miracles, repentance

DIRECTOR'S TIPS: For this storymime script, it might be helpful if the person doing the actions has some experience in mime, theater, or just likes acting goofy. The storytellers could be either boys or girls.

With this type of storytelling one person serves as the primary storyteller and the other person does the actions or shows the emotions of the characters and events in the story. The speaking storyteller pauses after every action verb to allow time for her partner to act out what's happening in the story. Suggested actions are included.

Invite the audience to imitate, or "mime," the actions after the silent storyteller has performed them. This is a great way to include audience participation and works especially well with five- to ten-year olds. When doing this, just remember to have your reader wait long enough for the children to perform each action before continuing reading the next section.

The storytellers could be either boys or girls. Both readers begin onstage or enter together. Bring up the stage lights and then begin when the students are quiet.

STORYTELLER 1	STORYTELLER 2
God's people weren't trusting in him or acting the way they should.	*Make a mean face. Mean stance. Hold up your fists for a fight!*
So, for three years God didn't let it rain on the land,	*Hold out your hand like you're waiting for rain.*
And the people were very thirsty.	*Act hot, sweaty, and thirsty.*
So, God's prophet Elijah went before the king.	*On one knee, as though approaching a king's throne.*
And then the king said, "You troublemaker, Elijah! What do you want?"	*Wag your finger accusingly.*
But Elijah wasn't intimidated.	*Place hands on hips, look confident.*
He told the king that he was really the troublemaker	*Point accusingly and wag your finger.*
And he challenged King Ahab's false prophets to a showdown on Carmel Mountain.	*Point to the mountain.*
So Ahab gathered together all his prophets and they headed up the mountain.	*Grab handholds and climb a mountain.*
Elijah asked the people, "How long are you going to wait to decide?"	*Hold out your hands, palms up, as if you're asking a question.*
"Who will you follow, God . . . or Baal?"	*Point to heaven when the storyteller says "God" and down when he says "Baal."*
But they stood there and didn't say anything.	*Stand, stare into space, and look stupid.*
Elijah said, "The God who sends fire is the true God!"	*Wave your hands as if you're a magician, making an explosion happen in front of you.*
So the people brought two bulls.	*Use your fingers and make little horns on your head.*
The 450 prophets of Baal cut up one bull into bite-sized hamburgers.	*Chop with your hands and pretend to eat a hamburger.*
They called to their god, Baal, and danced wildly to get his attention while Elijah watched and laughed.	*Stare forward, point, and laugh.*
But nothing happened because their god wasn't real.	*Shake your head no.*
Finally, in the evening, Elijah gathered the people together.	*Gesture as if you're gathering people for a huddle.*

The Barbecue on Carmel Mountain

He piled twelve stones into an altar,	*Pick up large imaginary boulders and pile them high.*
Dug a trench,	*Grab a shovel and dig a hole.*
Piled wood on top of the altar,	*Stack wood onto your imaginary altar.*
Cut his cow up into bite-sized hamburgers,	*Chop up the cow.*
And set them on the wood.	*Set the hamburgers on the wood. Eat a couple of hamburgers if you're hungry.*
Then he had the people pour four large jars of water on the hamburgers.	*Tip a large pitcher of water on your altar. Repeat four times. As they pour, count aloud, "1 . . . 2 . . . 3 . . . 4."*
And four more.	*Pour four more. Start getting tired. As they pour, count aloud, "1 . . . 2 . . . 3 . . . 4."*
And four more.	*Pour four more. By now you're exhausted. As they pour, count aloud, "1 . . . 2 . . . 3 . . . 4." Pour the last one on the other storyteller.*
Then Elijah prayed that God would prove himself to the people.	*Clasp your hands and close your eyes to pray.*
At once, fire flashed down from heaven and burned up the hamburgers,	*Make lightning with your hand and strike the wood. Let's hear the explosion!*
And the fire burned up the wood and even the stones and the water and the sand nearby.	*Warm your hands in front of a campfire.*
The people fell on their faces and cried, "The Lord is God! The Lord is God!"	*Put your hands out, bow down, and say, "The Lord is God! The Lord is God!"*
Then the prophets of Baal were punished.	*Karate chop with your hands.*
And God sent rain on the land.	*Wiggle your fingers and bring them down from the sky.*
And everyone in the land knew that the Lord was the one true God.	*Hold your hands up as if to worship God.*
The end.	*Take a bow.*

The Barbecue on Carmel Mountain

THE COURAGEOUS BEAUTY QUEEN (ESTHER)

BASED ON: Esther

BIG IDEA: Esther's story shows us that God is faithful and works behind the scenes in everyday life to deliver and bless his people.

BACKGROUND: King Xerxes and the Persians had conquered the Israelites and led them into captivity. One night, King Xerxes banished his queen. After a nationwide search, he chose a Jewish girl named Esther to be the new queen. God used her courage to protect Jews throughout the empire.

CAST: Bonnie—A slightly more serious storyteller trying to tell the story (girl or boy)
George—Her friend, who occasionally gets things mixed up (boy or girl)

Note: These names are used only for the purpose of clarity in the script. You may wish to use the actual names of the two storytellers as you present the story.

PROPS: Four signs with words large enough for the audience to read easily. The sign for Esther reads, "Hooray!" The sign for Haman reads, "Boo!" The sign for Mordecai reads, "Mordecai's a cool guy!" The sign for the king reads, "Long live the king!"

On the back of each card, write the name of the person to whom that card refers so that the storytellers can quickly find the appropriate card. You'll also need a table on which to lay the cards.

TOPICS: Choices, conviction, courage, family relationships, following God, hope, purpose

DIRECTOR'S TIPS: Sometimes George will hold up the wrong card. Because of this he needs to really nail the timing of his lines and be very aware of which card he will be holding up next. To assist the storytellers, the card names are underlined in the script.

To help with the flow of the story, the person who holds up a sign is typically the next person to speak.

This skit will work best with one boy and one girl acting as the storytellers. Both will start onstage or enter together. Bring up the stage lights and then begin when the students are quiet.

Teacher: **Lights! . . . Camera! . . . Action!**

George: *(To the audience)* **For today's story we're going to need your help!**

Bonnie: **That's right. You see, at certain points in the story, we'll hold up these cards** *(Point to the cards)* **and when we do, you'll say what's on that card!**

George: **Let's practice. At certain places in the story we'll be talking about a girl named Esther. When we do, we'll hold up this card** *(Hold up Esther's card).* **And when we do, we want everyone to cheer and say "Hooray!"**

Bonnie: **Great. And when we're talking about this guy named Haman—he was the bad guy—we'll hold up this card and we want you all to say, "Boo!"** (*Hold up* Haman's *card*)

George: **Good job. There's also a man in this story named Mordecai. His name rhymes with "pour the pie."**

Bonnie: **Pour the pie? What are you talking about? What on earth is that supposed to mean?**

George: **I don't know. It just rhymes with Mordecai. So does "Florida sky." Here's his card.** (*Hold up* Mordecai's *card and let them practice saying, "Mordecai's a cool guy!"*) **Oh, yeah! And for Mordecai you can also give us two big thumbs up. Let's try it again** (*Hold up the card again*). **Great!**

Bonnie: **Finally, there's one last card. This is the card for the king. And whenever we hold up this sign, you'll say, "Long live the king!" Ready?** (*Hold up the* king's *card and let them practice*)

George: **Well,** (*insert the name of the other storyteller*) _____, **do you think they're ready for the story?**

Bonnie: **I sure do. Let's get started!**

George: **Once upon a time there was this king,**

Bonnie: (*Hold up the* king's *card and let the audience respond, then set it down*) **Who wasn't too kind to his wife.**

George: **One night, to teach her a lesson, he kicked her out of the castle.**

Bonnie: (*As the king*) **"Oh, no! I'll be so lonely. I need a new queen! What will I do?"**

George: **So, he called in his advisors. They told him to hold a beauty pageant to find a new queen. One of his advisors was a man named Haman.**

Bonnie: (*Hold up* Haman's *card and let the audience respond, then set it down*) **Well, the king liked the idea of a beauty pageant to find a new bride.**

George: **I mean, who wouldn't?!**

Bonnie: **What did you say?**

George: **Nothing. Never mind.**

Bonnie: **And eventually, they came to the town of Susa where a beautiful Jewish girl lived. Her name was Esther.**

George: (*Hold up* Esther's *card and let the audience respond, then set it down*) **She lived there with her cousin. His name was Mordecai.**

Bonnie: (*Hold up* Mordecai's *card and let the audience respond, then set it down*) **Now, the men who'd been sent by the king were so impressed by the beauty of that Jewish girl, Esther,**

George: (*Hold up* Esther's *card and let the audience respond, then set it down*) **That they asked her to come back with them to the palace.**

Bonnie: **And the moment the king laid eyes on her, he knew he wanted to marry her.**

George: **Woo! Hubba. Hubba.**

Bonnie: **Now, her cousin, Mordecai,**

George: (*Hold up* Mordecai's *card and let the audience respond, then set it down*) **Refused to bow down to honor that evil man, Haman.**

Bonnie: (*Hold up* Haman's *card and let the audience respond, then set it down*) **So, that cruel advisor cooked up a plan. He convinced his boss, the king,**

George: (*Hold up the* king's *card and let the audience respond, then set it down*) **To set a date and announced that, on that day, everyone could kill the Jews.**

Bonnie: **He did this because he knew his enemy was a Jew.**

George: **And his enemy was a man named Mordecai.**

Bonnie: (*Hold up* Mordecai's *card and let the audience respond, then set it down*) **But he didn't know that the queen herself was Jewish. So, when her cousin found out, he sent word to the queen. You remember her name. It was Queen Esther!**

George: *(Hold up Mordecai's card and let the audience respond, then set it down)*

Bonnie: **I said it was Queen Esther!**

George: **Oh, right.** *(Hold up the king's card and let the audience respond, then set it down)*

Bonnie: **You're getting mixed up here. The queen's name was Esther!**

George: **Gotcha.** *(Hold up Esther's card upside down and let the audience respond, then set it down)*

Bonnie: **And he asked her to go and ask her husband to spare the lives of the Jews. As you remember, her husband was the king,**

George: *(Hold up the king's card and let the audience respond, then set it down)* **But there was a little problem.**

Bonnie: **Actually, a big problem.**

George: **You see, if you walked into the king's throne room without being invited in, there was some good news and some bad news.**

Bonnie: **The good news was that he would help you lose weight.**

George: **The bad news was that it was the ten pounds you carry around on top of your shoulders.** *(Draw finger across throat in a threatening gesture.)*

Bonnie: **What should she do? He might have her killed!**

George: **But at last, urged on by her cousin, she decided to trust her God.**

Bonnie: **And so, she went before the king.**

George: *(Hold up the king's card and let the audience respond, then set it down)* **She requested that he attend a special party she was planning. And she also invited Haman,**

Bonnie: *(Hold up Haman's card and let the audience respond, then set it down)* **At that party, she invited them both to yet another party. Oh, they were so excited. But finally, the queen—**

George: **Esther—** *(Hold up Mordecai's card and let the audience respond, then set it down)*

Bonnie: **You did it again.**

George: **How careless of me.**

Bonnie: **Said, "Oh, please save us! There is a cruel man who wants all Jews killed!"**

George: **And her husband demanded to know who it was.**

Bonnie: **"It's him!" she cried. "It's the cruel Haman!"**

George: *(Hold up Haman's card and let the audience respond, then set it down)* **And, when her husband heard that, he was furious!**

Bonnie: **He ordered that the traitor be killed and he gave his job to someone who deserved it a lot more: the noble and wise Mordecai!**

George: *(Hold up Mordecai's card and let the audience respond, then set it down)* **And since that time, Jews all over the world have celebrated a party every year.**

Bonnie: **In honor of that beautiful Queen Esther!**

George: *(Hold up the king's card and let the audience respond, then set it down)*

Bonnie: **I said, Esther.**

George: **Oh.** *(Hold up Mordecai's card and let the audience respond, then set it down)*

Bonnie: **Esther!** *(Reach over and pick up Esther's card. Hold it up, let the audience respond, then set it down)* **The End!—**

George: *(Quickly hold up Haman's card and let the audience respond, then set it down)*

Bonnie: **We're done now.**

George: *(Hold up Haman's card and let the audience respond, then set it down)*

Bonnie: **C'mon, let's go. Put down the cards. I don't have anything left to say.**

The Courageous Beauty Queen

George: *(Hold up Esther's card and let the audience respond, then set it down)*

Bonnie: **All right, that's enough. C'mon. Let's go.**

George: *(Hold up the king's card and let the audience respond, then set it down)*

Together: **The end.**

(Bow. Fade out the stage lights. Exit.)

UNIDENTIFIED FLYING ANGELS
(JESUS' BIRTH)

BASED ON: Luke 2:1-20

BIG IDEA: God sent his Son into the world to become our Savior.

BACKGROUND: When Jesus was born, the first people who found out about it (besides Mary and Joseph!) were the shepherds watching over their flocks of sheep. The shepherds quickly spread the news about Jesus' birth and everyone who heard it was impressed and amazed (Luke 2:20). The promised Messiah had finally arrived.

CAST: Ben-David—A shepherd on his way to worship the baby Jesus (boy or girl)
Les Braincell—A corny, bumbling, overenthusiastic detective investigating strange lights over Bethlehem (boy)

PROPS: Trench coat, notepad, magnifying glass for Les

TOPICS: Angels, Christmas, God's love, hope, Jesus, listening, prophecy fulfillment, witnessing, worship

DIRECTOR'S TIPS: Les Braincell's character is meant to be corny, so have your reader ham it up, be goofy, exaggerated, and silly. Since he appears in several skits, you may wish to use the same costume each time he makes an appearance.
During parts of this story, Les Braincell sings his own version of lines from the song "I've Been Working on the Railroad" (the "someone's in the kitchen with Dinah" part). Make sure he's familiar with these phrases and with the tune before beginning the story.
Les starts the scene onstage. Bring up the lights and then begin when the students are quiet.

Teacher: **Lights! . . . Camera! . . . Action!**

Les: **I'm Les, Les Braincell here, the world's greatest detective, here in Bethlehem, where strange things have been seen in the night sky.** *(Pull out a magnifying glass and look through it.)*

Ben-David: *(Enter)*

Les: *(See Ben-David through your magnifying glass)* **Aha!!! Are you a clue?**

Ben-David: **Nope. I'm a shepherd.**

Les: **A shepherd, huh?**

Ben-David: **Yes.**

Les: **Then you're an expert on sheep?**

Ben-David: **Of course.**

Les: **You know all about lambs?**

Ben-David: **Yes, I do.**

Les: **Then what did Mary have?**

Ben-David:	A little baby.
Les:	No! A little lamb! Whose fleece was white as . . .
Ben-David:	Swaddling clothes.
Les:	No! Snow! And everywhere that Mary went . . .
Ben-David:	Um, Mary hasn't gone anywhere. She's still in the stable.
Les:	She's unstable! Don't worry, I'll protect you! I'm an expert in four types of martial arts. (Do some karate moves.)
Ben-David:	Mary is in the stable with Joseph.
Les:	(Singing to the tune of "I've Been Working on the Railroad," the "someone's in the kitchen with Dinah" part. Get funky as you sing) Mary's in the stable with Joseph, Mary's in the stable, I know-oh-oh-oh. Mary's in the stable with Joseph, strummin' on the old banjo!
Ben-David:	Um, she's not strummin' on the old banjo.
Les:	Tuba?
Ben-David:	Listen. Mary's in the stable and had a baby tonight. She just got here from out of town.
Les:	Aha!!! Where's she from?
Ben-David:	She's from Nazareth, where she and Joseph live.
Les:	(Suspiciously) But yet, they've come here tonight, singing "fee-fi-fiddle-ee-i-o." There's something very weird going on around here.
Ben-David:	(Looking at Les) You could say that again.
Les:	(Beginning to repeat himself) But yet, they've come here tonight, singing "fee-fi-fiddle—"
Ben-David:	Look, I'm going to visit them right now. Do you want to come along?
Les:	I can't. I'm on duty. Looking for clues about the aliens who just arrived.
Ben-David:	Maybe it was the angels.
Les:	(Intensely) Angels? Are you serious? Don't play games with me here, man! Where's the proof? Where's the evidence? Where's the DNA?
Ben-David:	Angels don't have DNA.
Les:	Hmm . . . Do they have pet aliens?
Ben-David:	All I know is we were in the field watching over our sheep—
Les:	—Aha!!! There you go again, impersonating a shepherd.
Ben-David:	I am a shepherd.
Les:	(Thoughtfully) Then I must be impersonating someone. Maybe a private eye. Maybe I'm not who I say I am. Maybe I'm really Tom Cruise (or another movie star or popular sports celebrity) in disguise.
Ben-David:	I doubt it.
Les:	OK. So what did the angels say?
Ben-David:	They said our Savior has been born tonight in Bethlehem.
Les:	Aha!!!
Ben-David:	Aha what? Why did you say "aha?"
Les:	Because if sounds like I'm actually discovering something.
Ben-David:	Oh. And then the angels sang a song of praise to God.
Les:	Were the angels riding in UFOs?
Ben-David:	I don't think so. So, do you want to come with me or not?
Les:	(Accusingly) Yes, I do. What do you have to say about that?
Ben-David:	Aha!!!

Unidentified Flying Angels

Les:	You can't say that, it's my line.
Ben-David:	Um, try not to scare the baby, OK? *(Lead Les to another part of the stage, then point to the imaginary baby Jesus)* There he is. God's own Son.
Les:	He doesn't look like an alien to me.
Ben-David:	You don't have a clue, do you?
Les:	Nope, I'm completely clueless . . . But that sure is one special baby.
Ben-David:	You're right about that, Les. You're right about that. In fact, that's what the shepherds thought too, and they told everyone they met that their Savior had been born.
Les:	Sounds like something for all of us to do—even if we're not aliens.
Ben-David:	It sure does.
Together:	The end.

(Bow. Fade out the stage lights. Exit.)

THE DAY JESUS STAYED BEHIND
(JESUS AT THE TEMPLE)

BASED ON: Luke 2:41-52

BIG IDEA: Even from an early age Jesus put God's kingdom and God's priorities first.

BACKGROUND: We don't know much about Jesus' childhood. Luke tells us the only story about Jesus as a young man. When Jesus was twelve years old, his mother and Joseph took him to the Temple to celebrate the Jewish Passover. But when his family left without him, Jesus stayed behind learning about and teaching God's Word.

CAST: Mary—the mother of Jesus who lost track of him when she left for home after a busy week in Jerusalem (girl)
Les Braincell—A corny, bumbling, overenthusiastic detective investigating a trespassing accusation (boy)

PROPS: Trench coat, notepad, magnifying glass for Les

TOPICS: Family relationships, following God, God's Word, Jesus, priorities, purpose

DIRECTOR'S TIPS: Les Braincell's character is meant to be corny, so encourage your reader to ham it up, and be goofy, exaggerated, and silly. Since he appears in several skits, you may wish to use the same costume each time he makes an appearance.
    Both storytellers start onstage. Bring up the lights and then begin when the students are quiet.

Teacher: **Lights! . . . Camera! . . . Action!**

Les: **I'm Les, Les Braincell here, the world's greatest detective. I'm on a case here in Jerusalem interviewing Mary—Um, what did you say your last name is?**

Mary: **I didn't.**

Les: **All right, Mrs. Ididn't. Where were—**

Mary: *(Interrupting him)* **—No, no. I mean I didn't tell you my last name.**

Les: **Aha!!! So you want me to guess it, huh? Smith? . . . No, Dingleheimer . . . Wait, wait, I'll get it . . . Mary, Mary . . . Quite-contrary-how-does-your-garden-grow! That's it!**

Mary: **I don't have a last name.**

Les: *(Suspiciously)* **You don't have a last name? Are you in disguise?**

Mary: **Last names haven't been invented yet.**

Les: **Neither have bologna sandwiches.**

Mary: Most people just call me Mary, the mother of Jesus; or Mary, the wife of Joseph. Some people call me Mary, full of grace.

Les: OK, Mary the mother of Joseph, can you tell us what happened here today?

Mary: I'm the mother of Jesus, not Joseph; Joseph's my husband. And all three of us were here in Jerusalem.

Les: Aha!!! Just as I suspected! It's all coming together!

Mary: What's coming together?

Les: I have no idea.

Mary: Oh.

Les: So, you have a son!

Mary: Of course I have a son. That's why they call me the mother of Jesus.

Les: Exactly my point. So what happened to the boy?

Mary: Well, he disappeared.

Les: Aha!!! So, he's a magician.

Mary: No, he's not a magician. But the boy just disappeared.

Les: Whose boy?

Mary: My boy.

Les: You have a boy?

Mary: Jesus. God's son.

Les: I thought you said he was your son.

Mary: I did. He is.

Les: Are you claiming to be God?!

Mary: No, look, it's a long story. He's both my son and God's son, but I'm not God. I'm just Mary.

Les: The mother of Jesus.

Mary: Right.

Les: So what happened when he disappeared? Did you call 911?

Mary: No.

Les: Did you contact the FBI?

Mary: Um, no.

Les: Hire a private detective? Radio for help? Bring in the crime lab?

Mary: No—

Les: (Getting carried away, shaking her) —Why not, woman! What's wrong with you? This is your son we're talking about here! Your son goes missing and you don't even call the police?! What kind of a mother are you? Answer me!

Mary: But none of that stuff has been invented yet.

Les: It hasn't?

Mary: Nope. Police don't exist and neither do the FBI, crime labs, or 911.

Les: Hm. Maybe I don't exist either. Maybe I'm just a figment of my own imagination.

Mary: I doubt that.

Les: Well then, when he went missing, what did you do?

Mary: We looked for him. We looked all over for him.

Les: Did you check with mall security?

Mary: No. We searched with all our relatives, though. We thought maybe he was with someone else in their—

Les: —Minivan.

Mary: No, caravan.

Les: Caravan?

Mary: Yeah.

The Day Jesus Stayed Behind

Les: Dodge or Plymouth?

Mary: Camel.

Les: Oh. And? So what did you do then?

Mary: We didn't find him so went back to Jerusalem to look.

Les: (Getting carried away again) Well where was he? Did you ever find him? Don't keep me in suspense any longer! Tell me! I can't take it anymore! Ah!

Mary: Are you OK?

Les: No, I'm Les. Les Braincell, the world's greatest detective. Who are you?

Mary: Most people just call me Mary, the mother of—wait a minute. We went through this already.

Les: Just testing you.

Mary: Oh, well, anyway, my son was at the Temple.

Les: What?!

Mary: At the Temple.

Les: Your kid was at the Temple for three days?

Mary: Uh-huh.

Les: Was it like a lock-in or something?

Mary: No, but when I found him I was really angry. I said, "What do you think you're doing here? We've been looking all over for you!"

Les: Aha!!! And what did he say?

Mary: Well, he said, "Why were you looking for me? Didn't you know that I'd have to be here, in my Father's House?"

Les: His father lived in the church? What—was he the janitor?

Mary: His father was God.

Les: Oh, yeah. Right. I don't understand.

Mary: Well, we didn't really understand either. I mean, I knew he was a special child sent from God. But it took me most of my life to really understand what all that meant.

Les: (Writing notes) Ah . . . Very interesting.

Mary: And he was always obedient to us. And he grew smarter and stronger and friendlier and closer to God every day.

Les: Well, I guess that about wraps up this case . . . Jesus is no longer missing! So, where is Jesus now?

Mary: It's a long story . . . C'mon, I'll fill you in . . .

Together: The end.

(Bow. Fade out the stage lights. Exit.)

The Day Jesus Stayed Behind

THE MAN WHO ATE GRASSHOPPERS

(JOHN THE BAPTIST)

BASED ON:	Matthew 3; 11:1-19
BIG IDEA:	John the Baptist boldly prepared the way for Jesus' ministry.
BACKGROUND:	John the Baptist was Jesus' friend and cousin. One time Jesus called him the greatest man who ever lived (Matthew 11:11). John's ministry involved confronting people with their sin and teaching them how to live for God. He baptized people in the Jordan River when they repented.
	When John was imprisoned, he sent some of his followers to ask if Jesus really was the promised Messiah. Some Bible scholars think John was going through a period of questioning and doubt; others believe John sent his followers so that Jesus could reassure them. Either way, Jesus held John in high regard, and John the Baptist played a crucial role in preparing the way for Jesus' ministry. John the Baptist was truly one of God's heroes.
CAST:	Bonnie—A slightly more serious storyteller trying to tell the story (girl or boy)
	George—Her friend, who occasionally gets things mixed up (boy or girl)
	Note: These names are used only for the purpose of clarity in the script. You may wish to use the actual names of the two storytellers as you present the story.
PROPS:	None
TOPICS:	Baptism, conversion, doubt, faith, faithfulness, God's existence, God's Word, hope, Jesus, ministry, purpose, repentance
DIRECTOR'S TIPS:	The readers could be either boys or girls. Both readers start onstage or enter together. Bring up the stage lights and then begin when the students are quiet.

Teacher:	**Lights! . . . Camera! . . . Action!**		Bonnie:	**No.**
Bonnie:	**Today's story is about John the Baptist.**		George:	**Presbyterian?**
George:	**He baptized people who turned to God. That's why they called him John the Baptist.**		Bonnie:	**No, no, no. Listen, he prepared the way for Jesus to arrive.**
Bonnie:	**Not because he was a Baptist.**		George:	**Right. And he lived in the desert near the Jordan River.**
George:	**Since he was a Lutheran.**		Bonnie:	**And wore a leather belt and clothes made of camel hair. And he ate honey,**

George: Yummy!

Bonnie: And grasshoppers.

George: Yummy—wait, did you just say grasshoppers?

Bonnie: Uh-huh.

George: He ate grasshoppers?

Bonnie: Oh, yeah.

George: (To audience) Baptist Fear Factor.

Bonnie: The people came out to see him.

George: No kidding. How much did they pay to watch him eat the grasshoppers?

Bonnie: They didn't pay anything. They came from all over the area to listen to him preach.

George: I would've come for the grasshopper bit.

Bonnie: John was a special man whom God was using to prepare people's hearts to hear about Jesus. One day when John saw Jesus, he said, "Look! It's the Lamb of God who takes away the sin of the world!"

George: I'll bet Jesus wasn't too happy about that.

Bonnie: Why not?

George: Well, he called him Lamb-Man. Who wants to be called a lamb?

Bonnie: Jesus.

George: Oh.

Bonnie: Because he would be sacrificed for the sins of the whole world, just like the Jews used to sacrifice lambs so that God's anger would pass over them.

George: Gotcha.

Bonnie: Then Jesus let John baptize him and Jesus started to preach and teach people about God.

George: Now I remember! One day the king took someone else's wife to live with him as if they were married.

Bonnie: Yes. And John started telling people that the king's actions were wrong.

George: The king didn't like that one bit.

Bonnie: So he had John thrown into prison.

George: Where there were lots of bugs for him to snack on.

Bonnie: While he was in prison John sent his friends to ask Jesus if he really was the Savior.

George: He didn't know? How could he not know? Didn't he say, "This is the Lamb of God who takes away the sin of the world?"

Bonnie: Yeah.

George: Then why did he doubt?

Bonnie: Think about it. He was in prison. He was lonely. He was hungry.

George: He'd run out of grasshoppers. Good point.

Bonnie: So Jesus pointed to the Bible's promises about the Savior that God had promised to send. Jesus said, "Do the blind see?"

George: Yup.

Bonnie: "Do the lame walk?"

George: Yup.

Bonnie: "Are the sick cured? Do the deaf hear? Are the dead raised to life?"

George: Yup, yup, yup.

Bonnie: "Is the good news preached to the poor?"

George: Yuuuuuuuuuuup.

Bonnie: Is that all you can say?

George: Nope.

Bonnie: What else do you say?

George: Grasshoppers.

The Man Who Ate Grasshoppers

Bonnie: (After a sigh) **Then Jesus said, "Go tell John that God blesses those who aren't offended by me."**

George: **So they went to tell John the news.**

Bonnie: **After they'd left, Jesus told his followers that John the Baptist—**

George: **—Was really a Methodist in disguise.**

Bonnie: **He told them John was the greatest man who ever lived.**

George: **Whoa.**

Bonnie: **Now, while John was in prison, the king threw a great party and his daughter danced.**

George: (Act like a belly dancer)

Bonnie: (Watching George) **Hmm.**

George: **Did she dance like this?** (Dance some more)

Bonnie: **I sure hope not . . . And the king was so proud of her he said, "I'll give you anything you want!"**

George: (Talking like a teenage girl) **"Like, that is so cool! Lemme see, um . . . I want my own cell phone, and a cute little sporty sedan, and a credit card—"**

Bonnie: **—No. Her mom said to ask for John to be killed.**

George: **And for his head to be brought to her on a big plate.**

Bonnie: **That is very disgusting.**

George: **So they did.**

Bonnie: **Yuck.**

George: **Yup.**

Bonnie: **John is a good example of a man who spent his whole life dedicated to God. And Jesus honored him.**

George: **We should follow John's example.**

Bonnie: **Yes.**

George: **Dedicate ourselves to God.**

Bonnie: **Yes.**

George: **And eat lots of grasshoppers.**

Bonnie: **I knew you were going to say that.**

George: **Did you like my belly dancing?**

Bonnie: **Don't quit your day job.**

Together: **The end.**

(Bow. Fade out the stage lights. Exit.)

The Man Who Ate Grasshoppers

The Man Who Slept in Graves

(Jesus Heals a Demon-possessed Man)

BASED ON: Mark 5:1-20

BIG IDEA: Jesus is more powerful than demons. When Jesus sets us free, we're motivated to follow him too, just like the ex-demoniac.

BACKGROUND: Mark records the gripping account of how Jesus cast the demons out of a man who lived among the tombs. When the man was set free from the demons, he wanted to stay with Jesus, but Jesus told him to go home and tell his family about all that God had done for him. The man became the first Christian missionary to the Decapolis, ten cities in the region of the Gerasenes.

CAST: Peter—A friend of Jesus who watched him cast out demons (boy)
                     Demoniac—A man possessed with many demons that Jesus cast out (boy)

PROPS: None, or you may wish to have two musician's stools onstage. Have the storytellers seated on the stools for a portion of, or for the entire story.

TOPICS: Conversion, demons, following God, freedom, God's power, Jesus, new life, witnessing

DIRECTOR'S TIPS: This story is a little bit more serious and slightly scary. It would make a great campfire story at summer camp or at a lock-in for preteens. Because of its graphic content, use discernment in using this story with younger students.

The two storytellers will stay in character as Peter and the Demoniac throughout the entire story. Each person remains frozen while the other storyteller delivers his lines.

It's important that the Demoniac not act or sound silly when he's doing the demon voices. Those sections are mean to bring chills, not snickers. So, have your storytellers practice before beginning the presentation.

You may wish to have the storytellers sit on the stools, lean on them, or stand up and walk around at various parts in the story. The storytellers don't make eye contact with each other, but instead, each tells his own story to the audience.

Both readers start onstage or enter together. Bring up the stage lights and then begin when the students are quiet.

Teacher: **Lights! . . . Camera! . . . Action!**

Peter: **I was scared, I admit it. We all were. As our boat washed ashore, the mist was still rising off the water. Up ahead, tombs dotted the nearby hills. And that's when we heard the howling.**

Demoniac: **The days kinda run together in my mind. Days and months and years . . . Oh, they tried everything to help me, but nothing worked.**

Peter: **We climbed out of the boat and stepped onto the wet sand. I gulped as I listened to the strange sounds coming through the fog. I'd heard stories about the madman who lived up there in the hills—we'd all heard the stories.**

Demoniac: **They tried chaining me up but I broke through the chains. Eventually the people left me there alone to live in the graveyard among the graves and all the dead bodies.**

Peter: Then Jesus called to me, "Peter, tie up the boat; we're going ashore." And I said, "You want us to get out here? . . . By the tombs?"

Demoniac: Sometimes I'd slam my head against the tombstones or I'd just sit there slicing up my body with sharp rocks. Part of me was aware of what I was doing and tried to stop, but I couldn't—no matter how hard I tried. I wasn't in control of myself. Something else was.

Peter: They said it was demons that made him act the way he did. Nothing was strong enough to stop him. Night and day he would roam the hills, moaning and screaming. Attacking anyone who got in his way.

Demoniac: I was sitting in one of the open tombs, next to a rotting corpse, when they stepped ashore. I could sense that Jesus was nearby. And as I ran toward him, I knew that the demons inside of me wanted me to kill him.

Peter: I was next to the boat when he appeared out of the fog, howling like an animal, running straight toward Jesus. I thought he was going to attack him.

Demoniac: But I couldn't hurt him. Instead, I crumpled to the ground in front of him. I yelled at the top of my voice, "What do you want with me, Jesus, Son of the Most High God? Have you come to torture me?"

Peter: "Come out of this man, you evil spirit!" That's what Jesus said. "Come out of this man!" Jesus wasn't scared—not in the least. And then he asked him his name.

Demoniac: "Legion."

Peter: I knew it wasn't him talking, but the demons inside him.

Demoniac: "We are known as Legion, for we are many."

Peter: Then the demons begged the Lord over and over not to send them out of the region. They were scared of him—you could tell.

Demoniac: Nearby, there was a huge herd of pigs. Then the spirits inside of me asked Jesus to let them enter the pigs.

Peter: Jesus told the demons they could go, and suddenly the entire herd of pigs rushed down the steep cliffs and splashed into the lake. Every one of them drowned. Every last one.

Demoniac: The moment he said the word and the demons left I could feel the change. I was free—free for the first time in years! It was as if I was alive again. I had my life back!

Peter: The villagers couldn't believe their eyes, and neither could we. The man who'd been controlled by demons just a few minutes earlier was sitting at Jesus' feet dressed and thinking clearly.

Demoniac: The people were scared. They begged Jesus to leave. But I wasn't scared of him. For the first time in years I wasn't scared at all. And I didn't want him to leave. I wanted to stay with him, close by his side forever.

Peter: As we were getting back on the boat, the man asked if he could come along. But Jesus said, "No. Instead go home and tell your family what I've done for you."

Demoniac: So that's what I did. And that's what I'm still doing, telling everyone I meet how much he did for me. And everyone who heard about it is amazed at the power of this man of miracles. This man called Jesus.

(Bow. Fade out the stage lights. Exit.)

The Man Who Slept in Graves

NETS OF FISH
(THE MIRACULOUS FISH CATCH)

BASED ON: Luke 5:1-11

BIG IDEA: When we discover the true identity of Jesus, our lives are changed forever.

BACKGROUND: Even though the first disciples (Peter, Andrew, James, and John) had started to follow Jesus, they hadn't truly recognized who he really was. One day, after a miraculous catch of fish, they left their nets behind and followed Jesus for good. When we recognize the true identity of Christ, our lives are changed forever as well.

CAST: Bonnie—A slightly more serious storyteller trying to tell the story (girl or boy)
George—Her friend, who occasionally gets things mixed up (boy or girl)

Note: These names are used only for the purpose of clarity in the script. You may wish to use the actual names of the two storytellers as you present the story.

PROPS: None

TOPICS: Confession, following God, God's power, Jesus, ministry, purpose, sin

DIRECTOR'S TIPS: During the storymime section of this skit George should be enthusiastic about doing the actions, but keep going too far or doing the wrong ones. When Bonnie corrects him, he should nod or acknowledge that he understands. This acknowledgement is recorded in the script with the word "Oh."

Because of the nature of this storymime, it might work best to just have the silent storyteller do the actions rather than having the students join along.

The storytellers could be either boys or girls. Both readers start onstage or enter together. Bring up the stage lights and then begin when the students are quiet.

Teacher: **Lights! . . . Camera! . . . Action!**

Bonnie: **OK, for today's story, one of us will have to do the actions while the other one tells the story.**

George: **I'll do the actions.**

Bonnie: **Are you sure?**

George: **Absolutely.**

Bonnie: **You're not gonna mix them up or anything?**

George: **Me? Not a chance.**

Bonnie: **Are you sure?**

George: **Oh, yeah. No problemo. Where should I stand?**

Bonnie: **Um . . . You can stand right over there.**

George: *(Take one or two steps)* **Here?**

Bonnie: **Yeah.**

George: **OK.**

Bonnie: **You ready?**

George: **Yup.**

BONNIE	GEORGE
OK . . . One day, Peter and John were out fishing . . .	*Cast and reel as though using a fishing rod.*
With their nets.	**Oh.** *Toss nets toward audience.*
All night long.	*Yawn and continue to toss the nets.*
But they didn't catch anything.	*Fall asleep and snore.*
Um . . . they didn't fall asleep.	*Wake up and stretch your arms.*
In the morning, they were sitting on shore, cleaning and brushing their—	*Brush your teeth.*
—Nets. Brushing their nets.	**Oh.** *Brush off the nets with your toothbrush.*
Now, nearby Jesus was preaching to the crowds.	*Act like a dramatic preacher.*
The crowds were so big Jesus didn't have a place to stand.	*Repeat dramatic gestures; this time very tiny.*
So Peter let him stand on his boat.	*Rock back and forth and fall to the floor.*
I don't think it was that windy.	*Freeze.*
They pushed off from shore.	*Push off with an oar.*
And Jesus finished his sermon.	*Gesture wildly and then take a bow.*
After Jesus excused the crowd,	*Wave goodbye.*
He told Peter to drop the nets.	*Mime dropping a net on your feet. Hop around holding your foot.*
Not on his foot! Off the side of the boat . . .	*Drop the net off the side of the boat.*
Um, the other side of the boat.	*Drop the net off the other side of the boat.*
And the net began to fill with fish.	*Make fish lips and pretend to swim.*
Peter dropped to his knees and worshiped Jesus,	*Drop to your knees and clasp your hands in prayer.*

Nets of Fish

As the nets filled with fish.	*Make fish lips and pretend to swim. Swim up to Bonnie.*
Peter and the other disciples were amazed!	*Look completely shocked.*
The nets were so full the boats began to sink.	*Lean way over to one side.*
Not that much.	**Oh.** *Straighten up. As she looks away, tip over again.*
(Noticing George) I said, not that much . . .	*Straighten up again. As she looks away, tip over again.*
Peter rowed back to shore.	*Row.*
Um . . . shore is that way.	**Oh.** *Turn around and row again. Row into Bonnie; then tell her,* **Sorry. Too many waves.**
When they arrived onshore, they got out of the boat . . .	*Climb out of the boat.*
They left their nets full of fish . . .	*Drag your net a few feet and then leave it behind.*
And followed Jesus. And it changed their lives forever . . .	*Walk in place.*
The end.	*Bow.*

Bonnie: **Well, that wasn't too bad,** *(insert the name of the other storyteller)* **_____.**

George: **Wait a minute,** *(insert the name of the other storyteller)* **_____. Are you telling me they left their nets full of fish to follow Jesus?!**

Bonnie: **Uh-huh.**

George: **But they were fishermen! This was the catch of a lifetime! How could they do that?!**

Bonnie: **They had bigger fish to fry.**

George: **What are you talking about?**

Bonnie: **Jesus told them to fish for people, which means to bring people into his kingdom. He was calling them to a whole new way of life.**

George: **And they left their nets behind . . .**

Bonnie: **Yup. And when we follow Jesus, can you guess what we need to leave behind?**

George: **Hmm. Old ways of acting and thinking. Anything that might get in the way of us following Jesus.**

Bonnie: **Good job! But it's good to remember that we'll never be perfect.**

George: **And that's where his forgiveness comes in.**

Bonnie: **You got it.**

George: **Good. Now, you wanna go fishing?**

Bonnie: **Why not? As long as you promise not to mess things up.**

George: **Me? Not a chance . . .**

Together: **The end.**

(Bow. Fade out the stage lights. Exit.)

THE SONS OF THUNDER
(JAMES AND JOHN)

BASED ON: John 13:18-28; Acts 12:1, 2; Matthew 17:1-9; 1 John 3:18; and the life and writings of John the apostle

BIG IDEA: The apostle John loved Jesus. In his life and writings he emphasized how important it is to put love into action (1 John 3:18).

BACKGROUND: John and James were first-century fishermen who left their nets and their livelihood behind to become followers of Jesus. Although John and his brother James struggled with ambition, John eventually learned to humbly follow Jesus and began a new life marked by genuine love for others. John wrote five books of the Bible and was an important leader in the early Christian church.

CAST: Bonnie—A slightly more serious storyteller trying to tell the story (girl or boy)
George—Her friend, who occasionally gets things mixed up (boy or girl)

Note: These names are used only for the purpose of clarity in the script. You may wish to use the actual names of the two storytellers as you present the story.

PROPS: None

TOPICS: Following God, friendship, God's love, Jesus, priorities, witnessing

DIRECTOR'S TIPS: Throughout the skit George says, "The Sons of Thunnnnnnnnder!" Have him practice it before beginning so that he can do it in a voice similar to an announcer for All-Star Wrestling.
The readers could be either boys or girls. Both readers start onstage or enter together. Bring up the stage lights and then begin when the students are quiet.

Teacher: Lights! . . . Camera! . . . Action!

Bonnie: Today's story is about a man named John.

George: Both he and his brother, James,

Bonnie: Were two of Jesus' closest friends.

George: James and John.

Bonnie: John and James.

George: The sons of a guy named Zebedee.

Bonnie: Jesus called them the Sons of Thunder!

George: Sounds like they were professional wrestlers or something. (*Talking like a ringside announcer*) "Now entering the ring, the Sons of Thunnnnnnnnder!"

Bonnie: Jesus first asked John—

George: —And his brother, James—

Bonnie: To follow him one day when he saw them fixing their nets,

George: With their dad,

Bonnie: Zebedee. So, John—

George: —And his brother, James—The Sons of Thunnnnnnnnder!

Bonnie: Followed Jesus,

George: While Zebedee stayed in the boat.

Bonnie: And then, during their time with Jesus, John—

George: —And his brother, James

Bonnie: Had lots of adventures.

George: Camping with Jesus . . .

Bonnie: Listening to his stories . . .

George: Watching him cast out demons . . .

Bonnie: Walk on the water . . .

George: Heal the sick . . .

Bonnie: Raise the dead . . .

George: And do tons of other cool stuff.

Bonnie: But one of the most life-changing things that John—

George: —And his brother, James

Bonnie: Why do you keep doing that?

George: Well, they were brothers.

Bonnie: I know, but it's distracting. Every time I say "John," you say, "and his brother James." It's starting to annoy me.

George: Well, I'll have to watch that then.

Bonnie: Anyway, John—

George: —And his brother, James—

Bonnie: Stop it.

George: Okey-dokey.

Bonnie: So, John . . . *(wait for George to say something)* Aren't you going to say anything?

George: No, you didn't want me to.

Bonnie: OK, John . . . *(Pause again. You expect George to say it. Look at him.)*

George: Go on.

Bonnie: OK. Great. Wow. All right then. So, John—

George: —And his brother, James—The Sons of Thunnnnnnnnder!

Bonnie: I knew you were gonna do that.

George: Went with Jesus up a mountainside and,

Bonnie: Saw him in all his glory.

George: And he was really glow-y.

Bonnie: There was a bright, bright light. It was the glory of God.

George: Glow-y glory.

Bonnie: Right.

George: A glow-y glory, not a gory glory. Wow, say that five times fast. *(Give it a shot.)*

Bonnie: Then later, when Jesus was about to die, he asked John to take care of his mother, Mary.

George: John called himself the disciple whom Jesus loved.

Bonnie: He became an important leader in the early church.

George: And he was a humble and powerful servant of Christ.

Bonnie: That's right. And he shared the good news of salvation with many people,

George: Encouraged and challenged believers,

Bonnie: And wrote the book of John—

The Sons of Thunder

George: —And his brother, James.

Bonnie: Um, no. His brother James didn't write a book.

George: Why not?

Bonnie: King Herod had him killed.

George: Yikes.

Bonnie: So, besides the book of John, John also wrote first John,

George: Second John,

Bonnie: Third John,

George: Fourth John.

Bonnie: Um, there's no fourth John.

George: There isn't? OK, fifth John.

Bonnie: There's no fifth John either. Just a first, second, and third John. They're books of the Bible, OK? First, second, and third John.

George: And the book of John.

Bonnie: Right.

George: So that makes four Johns.

Bonnie: But we already counted that one.

George: And there's the book of Revelation. He wrote that too. That could be a fourth John or maybe a fifth John, if the first John was actually called first John and not just John.

Bonnie: It's Revelation, not fourth John or fifth John!

George: But it could be—

Bonnie: —Look, stop arguing about it. There are only three Johns!

George: And Revelation.

Bonnie: Right.

George: And John—

Bonnie: —That's right.—

George: —And his brother, James.

Bonnie: That's it! I'm getting a new storytelling partner!

George: You know, *(insert the name of the other storyteller)* _____, when we get to heaven I'd really like to meet John.

Bonnie: And his brother, James?

George: No, just John.

Bonnie: Oh. Are you sure?

George: Yup. Absolutely.

Bonnie: Good.

George: Just John . . . And maybe one other person . . . *(Wait for a long time)* His brother, James.

Bonnie: I knew you were gonna say that.

George: The Sons of Thunnnnnnnnder!

Together: The end.

(Bow. Fade out the stage lights. Exit.)

RAPPELLING THROUGH THE ROOF
(Jesus Heals a Paralyzed Man)

BASED ON: Mark 2:1-12

BIG IDEA: Jesus has the power to heal our bodies and forgive our sins.

BACKGROUND: Early in Jesus' ministry he was gaining notoriety because of his amazing power and unusual claims. In this story, he shows that he not only has power over physical disabilities and diseases but also the worst disease of all—sin. We also see that nothing should get in the way of our bringing our friends to Jesus.

CAST: Bonnie—A slightly more serious storyteller trying to tell the story (girl or boy)
George—Her friend, who occasionally gets things mixed up (boy or girl)

Note: These names are used only for the purpose of clarity in the script. You may wish to use the actual names of the two storytellers as you present the story.

PROPS: None

TOPICS: Faith, forgiveness, friendship, God's power, Jesus, priorities

DIRECTOR'S TIPS: The storytellers could be either boys or girls. Both readers start onstage or enter together. Bring up the stage lights and then begin when the students are quiet.

Teacher: **Lights! . . . Camera! . . . Action!**

Bonnie: **This is an amazing story.**

George: **It sure is!**

Bonnie: **This is one of the coolest and funniest and weirdest stories about Jesus.**

George: **That's right.**

Bonnie: **Do you even know what story I'm talking about?**

George: **Of course I do.**

Bonnie: **What story is it?**

George: **Um . . . it's the story of . . . um . . .**

Bonnie: **You don't have a clue, do you?**

George: **Not a one.**

Bonnie: **I didn't think so. Now, it happened in the city of Capernaum. Jesus had just arrived and word spread quickly.**

George: **Pretty soon, the news crews were out and everything.** (*Start hitting your chest alternately with each hand*)

Bonnie: **What are you doing?**

George: **Helicopter sounds.**

Bonnie:	Helicopter?
George:	Channel 12 News.
Bonnie:	I don't think Channel 12 News was there. But a big crowd of people had come, and there were so many people packed into the house that not even one more person could fit through the door.
George:	So they all got into the helicopter.
Bonnie:	Now, there were these four guys carrying their friend on a mat.
George:	Their friend's name was Matt.
Bonnie:	No, his name wasn't Matt. He was lying on a mat.
George:	Then I'm glad I'm not Matt.
Bonnie:	They were carrying one man on a mat. Not a person, a mat! Like a cot or a sleeping bag. And they tried to get in past the crowd of people.
George:	And the guy on the mat couldn't get up because there were too many people.
Bonnie:	Actually, he couldn't get up because he was paralyzed.
George:	He was?
Bonnie:	Yeah, and his friends were trying to bring him to Jesus. And they weren't going to let a little thing like a packed house get in the way.
George:	So what'd they do?
Bonnie:	They climbed up on the roof.
George:	Why didn't they just use the helicopter?
Bonnie:	There was no helicopter! And when they got up on the roof they began to dig a hole in it.
George:	What? Wait a minute. You're telling me they just started digging through the roof?

Bonnie:	Yup. Roofs were made of mud and tile back then, much easier to dig through. Then they tied ropes to the guy's mat.
George:	That had to hurt.
Bonnie:	Matt wasn't a person!
George:	What was he?
Bonnie:	A mat.
George:	Oh.
Bonnie:	Then the paralyzed man's friends started lowering him through the hole in the roof.
George:	So they lowered the guy down?
Bonnie:	Yup.
George:	That guy must have been scared out of his wits thinking, "If these guys aren't careful I might tip off this mat and land on the ground and break both my legs and be paralyzed for life!"
Bonnie:	He was already paralyzed for life.
George:	And Matt was about to be.
Bonnie:	They lowered him down, right in front of Jesus. And when Jesus saw what kind of faith the guy's buddies had, he was impressed and said, "Friend, your sins are forgiven."
George:	But I thought they brought him to get healed!
Bonnie:	They did, but Jesus was taking care of the most important thing first. It's much more important that we have faith and find forgiveness than whether or not we can walk around.
George:	Hmm . . . I've never thought of that before.
Bonnie:	Now, when all the Pharisees heard him say that—
George:	—What's a swimming ferret have to do with anything?
Bonnie:	What?

Rappelling Through the Roof

George: You said, "All the ferrets in the sea."

Bonnie: No. Pharisees. A Pharisee was a religious ruler in Jesus' day.

George: They weren't furry little animals?

Bonnie: No.

George: Oh.

Bonnie: They were people who were very concerned about following all the Jewish rules. And sometimes they forgot that our faith is what makes us right with God, not how well we meet a bunch of religious requirements.

George: I thought you said "ferrets."

Bonnie: I know.

George: A ferret is a little furry woodland creature.

Bonnie: Yes, I know that.

George: They don't have anything to do with healing paralyzed guys on mats.

Bonnie: No, they don't.

George: And they don't live in the oceans either.

Bonnie: Can I get on with the story now?

George: Yes. Pharisees. Very religious. Worried about rules. Gotcha.

Bonnie: So when they heard what Jesus said about forgiveness they thought, "Only God can forgive someone's sin!"

George: Huh. They were right about that.

Bonnie: Yes, they were. And since Jesus claimed to do it, they assumed he was claiming to be—

George: —God himself!

Bonnie: Right. Then Jesus said, "It's easier to heal bones than souls. But to show you that I can do the hard thing, I'll do the easy one too. Then you'll know that I really can forgive sins."

George: Lemme guess, Jesus told the guy, "Stand up. Pick up that mat of yours and go home."

Bonnie: Exactly. And then the man leapt to his feet, picked up his mat and began to push his way through the crowd.

George: Everyone there was amazed.

Bonnie: Right.

George: Especially Matt.

Bonnie: (Shake your head) Do you practice being this confused, or were you born this way?

George: I'm naturally gifted.

Bonnie: And the people began to praise and thank God. No one had ever seen anything like that before.

Together: The end.

(Bow. Fade out the stage lights. Exit.)

Rappelling Through the Roof

At the Scene of the Grave
(Jesus' Resurrection)

BASED ON:	Mark 16; John 20:1-18
BIG IDEA:	Three days after dying, Jesus rose from the dead, just as he'd predicted he would. He took our penalty on himself and rose so that we could know our sins are forgiven when we trust in him.
BACKGROUND:	Each of the Gospel writers records in his own words what happened at the scene of the empty tomb. Together, they give us a complete picture of the people to whom Jesus appeared after his resurrection. The best news of all is that Jesus rose from the dead so that we could have eternal life with God when we place our faith in Jesus Christ.
CAST:	Mary of Magdala—One of Jesus' followers and the first person to see Jesus alive after he rose from the dead (girl) Les Braincell—A corny, bumbling, overenthusiastic detective investigating the report of a missing body in a graveyard near Jerusalem (boy)
PROPS:	Trench coat, notepad, magnifying glass for Les
TOPICS:	Easter, God's love, grace, Jesus, new life, prophecy fulfillment
DIRECTOR'S TIPS:	Les Braincell's character is meant to be corny, so choose a reader who can ham it up and be goofy, exaggerated, and silly. Since he appears in several skits, you may wish to use the same costume each time he makes an appearance. Les starts the scene onstage. Bring up the lights and then begin when the students are quiet.

Teacher: Lights! . . . Camera! . . . Action!

Les: I'm Les, Les Braincell here, the world's greatest detective. I'm on the scene in this graveyard . . . *(looking around)* I don't like graveyards . . . But I'm not afraid.

Mary: *(Enter, Mary)* Boo.

Les: Ah! *(You're very scared!)* What are you doing, sneaking up on me like that! Who do you think you are?

Mary: Mary.

Les: Aha! Just as I suspected! Where were you on April 22 at 5:00 p.m.?

Mary: Um . . . I don't know . . .

Les: So you might have been stealing the body!

Mary: What body?

Les: Acting innocent, huh? Well, I can play that game too. I'm telling you, it wasn't me. I didn't do it!

Mary: Do what?

Les: Steal the candy from my mommy's jar when I was eight years old. OK, I admit it! You broke me! I can't take the pressure. I did it! I'm guilty! Take me away!

Mary: What are you talking about?

Les: Oh. *(Flipping open a notebook)* Nothing. So, what did you say your name is?

Mary: Mary of Magdala.

Les: What are you doing sneaking through a graveyard in the middle of the night?

Mary: It's not the middle of the night. It's daybreak.

Les: Trying to overwhelm me with details, huh? Well, it won't work! I'm as sharp as . . . as . . .

Mary: A marble?

Les: Right! Now, where were we?

Mary: In the graveyard.

Les: I don't like graveyards.

Mary: Boo.

Les: *(Totally frightened)* Ah!

Mary: Hee, hee, hee . . .

Les: Did you see a ghost?

Mary: No.

Les: So you admit it then!

Mary: Admit what?

Les: You admit that you didn't see a ghost! Now we're getting somewhere!

Mary: What are you talking about?

Les: I have no idea.

Mary: I didn't see any ghosts, but I did see a man.

Les: Was his name Les Braincell?

Mary: No.

Les: You mean I've changed my name?

Mary: I saw Jesus.

Les: So, you say you saw Jesus?

Mary: Yes, in the flesh, so to speak.

Les: And he was alive?

Mary: Yes.

Les: Was he carrying a dead body by any chance? Someone reported a missing body this morning.

Mary: Um . . . That was Jesus' body that was missing.

Les: So, now we have a missing person and a missing body. It's a good thing I'm here.

Mary: Why is that?

Les: Because I'm Les, Les Braincell, the world's greatest detective.

Mary: Oh. But Jesus isn't missing.

Les: He's not?

Mary: No. And no one stole his body.

Les: They didn't?

Mary: No. He came back from the dead.

Les: Aha!!! CPR!

Mary: Um, no. God brought him back to life.

Les: God performed CPR on a missing person?

Mary: No.

Les: So . . . It's all God's fault.

Mary: It's not God's fault, Mr. Braincell. Nothing went wrong. It was his plan all along.

Les: His plan, huh. So it was premeditated.

Mary: Look, I have to go.

At the Scene of the Grave

Les: Wait. So, you say Jesus is alive?

Mary: Yes!

Les: Well, you have to admit it's a little farfetched to believe that somebody's gonna be killed, dead as a doorknob, and then three days later come back to life.

Mary: That's right. It is farfetched. And that's why I'm so excited!

Les: Because it's the biggest news story of all time?

Mary: Exactly.

Les: Hmm . . . I don't like watching the news. It's too depressing.

Mary: Not this news. I'm on my way right now to tell John and Peter and the rest of Jesus' friends that he isn't dead, but alive—just as he said he would be. Wanna come?

Les: Absolutely. Then I can solve this case once and for all . . . Um, are you positive there aren't any ghosts out here?

Mary: Boo.

Les: *(Totally frightened)* Ah! Stop doing that!

Mary: Hee, hee, hee . . .

Together: The end.

(Bow. Fade out the stage lights. Exit.)

At the Scene of the Grave

THE FIRST CHRISTIAN MARTYR

(STEPHEN)

BASED ON: Acts 6:8—8:8

BIG IDEA: Stephen boldly stood up for Christ and shared the gospel with the Jews of his day. He is a great example of boldness and forgiveness.

BACKGROUND: After Pentecost the early Christian church experienced dynamic growth and unity. As the church grew, Stephen was chosen to help distribute food to the Grecian widows. He also preached the gospel. One day he was dragged to the High Priest and falsely accused of speaking against God.

After giving his defense, Stephen was stoned to death and became the first Christian martyr. The Bible describes Stephen as a man full of faith, God's grace, power, wisdom, and the Holy Spirit, who did great wonders and miraculous signs.

CAST: Bonnie—A slightly more serious storyteller trying to tell the story (girl or boy)
George—Her friend, who occasionally gets things mixed up (boy or girl)

Note: These names are used only for the purpose of clarity in the script. You may wish to use the actual names of the two storytellers as you present the story.

PROPS: None

TOPICS: Confession, courage, faith, following God, forgiveness, hope, ministry, prophecy fulfillment, witnessing

DIRECTOR'S TIPS: This story has a rhyming section that has a real beat to it. Before performing this skit, have your readers practice it so that they can nail that part when they do the skit in front of the class.

The storytellers could be either boys or girls. Both readers start onstage or enter together. Bring up the stage lights and then begin when the students are quiet.

Teacher: **Lights! . . . Camera! . . . Action!**

George: **After Jesus returned to heaven,**

Bonnie: **The Christian church grew quickly.**

George: **And Jesus' followers told many people he had risen from the dead.**

Bonnie: **The number of Christians increased,**

George: **And they shared everything together.**

Bonnie: **There were no needy people,**

George: **Or poor people,**

Bonnie: **Or rich people,**

George: **Or fat people or skinny people.**

Bonnie: **Um. There were fat and skinny people, but they did share everything they owned.**

George: Like meatloaf.

Bonnie: Um. Right.

George: Eventually, though, some widows

Bonnie: Were being left out and weren't getting their daily supply of—

George: —Meatloaf.

Bonnie: So, the group of disciples who'd been with Jesus,

George: Huddled up and talked it over.

Bonnie: "We're preachers, not waiters. We need other guys to hand out the food."

George: So they decided to choose seven men full of the Holy Spirit,

Bonnie: And full of wisdom.

George: This idea pleased everyone. One of the men they chose was named Stephen.

George: And once again, the church grew quickly.

George: Even Jewish priests became followers of Jesus.

Bonnie: And Stephen did wonders and miracles among the people.

George: But then, a group of Jews began to argue with him,

Bonnie: But they always lost their arguments,

George: Because of Stephen's wisdom,

Bonnie: And because of God's Spirit speaking through him.

George: So, they got some people to tell lies about Stephen.

Bonnie: They said he was speaking against God—

George: —And against Moses.

Bonnie: And the people turned against him.

George: They grabbed Stephen,

Bonnie: Brought him to their leaders, and told them that he was speaking against God.

George: The rulers looked at Stephen and waited for him to speak . . .

Bonnie:: Then the priest who was in charge said,

George: "Is it true you hand out meatloaf?"

Bonnie: Give me a break. He asked him, "Are these accusations true?"

George: And then Stephen took a deep breath . . .

Bonnie: Are you ready?

George: I think so.

(If desired, this next section could be done with a drum or rhythmic beat in the background.)

Bonnie: Stephen told them all a story that the men could understand.

George: Of how God had promised Abraham a wonderful land.

Bonnie: And how a man named Jacob had a dozen sons,

George: And the kid named Joseph was his favorite one.

Bonnie: But the brothers all hated that he was the "fave"—

George: —So they plotted,

Bonnie: And he ended up

Together: Sold as a slave!

George: In Egypt-land, God saved him indeed.

Bonnie: He was handing out food to the people in need!

George: He invited his family and they chilled in style.

Bonnie: Down in Egypt,

George: Near the river

Bonnie: Called the River Nile.

The First Christian Martyr

George:	Then their kids all grew, and they had a blast.
Bonnie:	Till a king came along who didn't know the past.
George:	So he made 'em all slaves,
Bonnie:	And he made 'em all sad,
George:	And Moses killed a guard when he got really mad.
Bonnie:	So Moses moved away and protected sheep,
George:	In the hills,
Bonnie:	And the mountains,
Together:	And the valleys deep!
George:	Till God sent him back! He set the people free!
Bonnie:	And he led all the Jews right across the sea.
George:	I said across the sea!
Bonnie:	I said across the sea!
George:	I said he led all the Jews right across the sea.
Bonnie:	Then Moses told the people in the desert one day,
George:	Of a prophet who would come,
Bonnie:	But they turned away;
George:	And they wouldn't obey.
Bonnie:	And they didn't come back to the Lord to pray.
George:	So the Lord let 'em do what they wanted to do.
Bonnie:	And the prophets wrote about it, so you know it's true.
George:	After Moses there was David—
Bonnie:	—And then David's son—
George:	And there's still the great promise of the Righteous One.
Bonnie:	You know he's the guy,
George:	That you sent to die,
Bonnie:	And I see him right now,
George:	Looking down from the sky!

(End of the rhythmic beat section.)

Bonnie:	When the leaders heard that,
George:	They were so angry,
Bonnie:	They screamed at the top of their lungs;

George:	Ah!
Bonnie:	Rushed toward Stephen,
George:	Err!
Bonnie:	Dragged him outside the city,
George:	And then threw stones at him.
Bonnie:	While they did that,
George:	Stephen prayed that God would forgive them.
Bonnie:	And then,
George:	Stephen died.
Bonnie:	That day, the believers were attacked,
George:	And Christians were scattered all over the land.
Bonnie:	They were very sad about Stephen being killed,
George:	But everywhere they went,
Bonnie:	They preached the good news about Jesus,
George:	Just as Stephen had.
Bonnie:	And God worked in mighty ways.
George:	Many people were healed,
Bonnie:	And set free from demons.
George:	The news about Jesus spread all around and many people became believers.
Bonnie:	So there was great joy in the land.
George:	And lots and lots of meatloaf.
Bonnie:	Oh, brother.
Together:	The end.

(Bow. Fade out the stage lights. Exit.)

Preacher to the World

(Paul)

BASED ON:	Acts 9:1-31; Romans 7:15-25; Galatians 1:17, 18; the life and writings of Paul (specific verses are referred to in the script)
BIG IDEA:	Paul passionately preached to the Gentiles and carried God's Word to the ends of the known world. His zeal for Christ and concern for right teaching can still inspire us today.
BACKGROUND:	Paul was one of the most passionate persecutors of the early Christian church, but one day after a dramatic conversion experience he became a Christian himself. After Paul's conversion, God sent him to preach the good news about Jesus to the Gentiles. He wrote or co-wrote thirteen books of the New Testament, and was one of the most influential Christians of all time.
CAST:	Paul of Tarsus—A convert to Christianity and God's chosen apostle to the Gentiles (boy) Les Braincell —A corny, bumbling, overenthusiastic detective investigating the report of a missing person on the road to Damascus (boy)
PROPS:	Trench coat, notepad, magnifying glass for Les
TOPICS:	Conversion, courage, following God, forgiveness, God's Word, grace, new life, purpose, witnessing
DIRECTOR'S TIPS:	Les Braincell's character is meant to be corny, so encourage your reader to ham it up, and be goofy, exaggerated, and silly. Since he appears in several skits, you may wish to use the same costume each time he makes an appearance. Les starts the scene onstage. Bring up the stage lights and then begin when the students are quiet.

Teacher: **Lights! . . . Camera! . . . Action!**

Les: **I'm Les, Les Braincell here, the world's greatest detective. I'm on this road looking for clues . . .** *(looking around through his magnifying glass as Paul enters)* **Aha!!! Are you a clue?**

Paul: **No, I'm a man. Paul. Can I help you?**

Les: **Do I look like I need your help?!** *(Look at him through your magnifying glass)*

Paul: **That would be a yes.**

Les: **Oh . . . Well, I don't need your help! I'm the world's greatest detective!** *(Search for your magnifying glass; it's in your left hand)* **By the way . . . have you seen my magnifying glass?**

Paul: **Um. It's in your hand.**

Les: Aha!!! So, you want to help me, huh? Well, according to my missing person's report . . . by the way, have you seen my missing person's report?

Paul: Nope. Maybe it's missing.

Les: Of course it is! That's why it's called a missing person's report! If I knew where it was it wouldn't be missing now, would it?

Paul: I suppose not.

Les: You'd know these things if you were the world's greatest detective.

Paul: I guess I would.

Les: So, according to my missing person's report, a man named Saul has been missing ever since a bright light shone on the road to Damascus. There was also a loud sound. I think we might be dealing with a case of alien abduction here.

Paul: Well, maybe I can help, then.

Les: Why? Are you an alien?

Paul: Yes.

Les: You're an alien? Well, that explains it. Wait a minute—did you just say you're an alien?

Paul: Yup. I'm an alien on this earth because I belong in another place.

Les: So do I. I'm from New Jersey.

Paul: Oh . . . Well, I belong in heaven. And I think I know what happened to that guy you're talking about.

Les: Oh? And what's that?

Paul: He's not missing.

Les: That's good.

Paul: He's dead.

Les: That's bad—He's dead! Murdered, you say?

Paul: No, but he died on the road to Damascus. I should know. I used to be him. You see, my name is Paul, but it used to be Saul.

Les: So, what do you do?

Paul: Well, even though I try my hardest, I don't always do what I want to do.

Les: You don't do what you want to do?

Paul: No. But I do do what I don't want to do.

Les: You do do what you don't want to do?

Paul: Right.

Les: And you don't do what you do want to do?

Paul: You got it.

Les: And when you do do what you don't want to do, and don't do what you do want to do, what do you do?—What in the world am I talking about?

Paul: My point is, when I met Jesus, my life was changed forever.

Les: How's that?

Paul: Now, I'm dead.

Les: You're what?!

Paul: I'm dead to sin. But I have a whole new life with God.

Les: So you were dead, and you're alive again?

Paul: Yup. And now I preach the good news about Jesus everywhere. Once, some people tried to kill me for doing it.

Les: And did they kill you?

Paul: How could I be telling you this if they killed me?

Les: Trying to confuse me with the obvious, huh?

Paul: I don't think I need to. You're doing that on your own.

Preacher to the World

Les:	Exactly my point! So, what did you do then?
Paul:	I got up and went to preach to them.
Les:	To whom?
Paul:	The people who tried to kill me.
Les:	You went to preach to the people who tried to kill you for preaching to them?!
Paul:	Yup.
Les:	Why would you do that?! They might have killed you!
Paul:	Oh, don't worry; that wouldn't have hurt me.
Les:	It wouldn't have hurt you? What are you talking about, man? Are you trying to say you'd be better off dead?
Paul:	Actually, yes. Then I'd be in heaven with Jesus.
Les:	You think you're good enough to get to heaven?!
Paul:	Not at all; not good enough at all. We only get to heaven by faith.
Les:	I see.
Paul:	So now, I serve God because he set me free. You might say I'm a slave to God.
Les:	You're a slave to God because he set you free?
Paul:	Right.
Les:	And you're alive, even though you're dead?
Paul:	Yup.
Les:	And you used to be someone else?
Paul:	You got it.
Les:	And you're an alien on this planet?
Paul:	Right.
Les:	You're not an alien, you're an idiot!
Paul:	Are you saying I'm a fool?
Les:	Yes!
Paul:	I'm glad you noticed.
Les:	What?
Paul:	The weaker I am and the more foolish I am, the more I need to rely on God. So I'm glad to be a fool. Thank you very much.
Les:	That's it! I'm taking you in. And, I'm gonna recommend that they send you away for a good long time. You're dangerous. You're schizophrenic, suicidal, paranoid, and downright nuts!
Paul:	Well, at least you've solved your case.
Les:	Yes, I have. Saul isn't missing; he just turned into Paul the apostle.
Paul:	Right.
Les:	(Leaning in close to Paul) So are you really an alien?
Paul:	In a certain way, yes.
Les:	Can I ride in your spaceship?
Paul:	I'm not that kind of alien. Come on, let's go. I'll tell you how you can become an alien too.
Les:	Oh goody, goody, goody. I've always wanted to have my own ray gun.
Together:	The end.

(Bow. Fade out the stage lights. Exit.)

When Tabitha Got Sew Sick
. . . She Dyed (Tabitha and Peter)

BASED ON:	Acts 9:36-43
BIG IDEA:	Through God's power, Peter raised Tabitha, a generous and faithful woman, back to life.
BACKGROUND:	Tabitha, a kindhearted woman who was generous to the poor, lived in Joppa. After she died, the disciples showed amazing faith by calling Peter to her home, apparently to have him raise her back to life—which he did. As a result, many people from that region believed in the Lord.
CAST:	Bonnie—A slightly more serious storyteller trying to tell the story (girl or boy)
	George—Her friend, who occasionally gets things mixed up (boy or girl)

Note: These names are used only for the purpose of clarity in the script. You may wish to use the actual names of the two storytellers as you present the story.

    This story will also include audience participation by eight people: a boy to be Peter, two people to be the doorway, two girls to be weeping widows, two people to be disciples, and a man or large boy to be Tabitha. The bigger Tabitha is, the funnier the scene will be.

PROPS:	None, only you may wish to have a wig for the person who plays the part of Tabitha
TOPICS:	Death, faith, generosity, God's power, grief and loss, new life, Peter
DIRECTOR'S TIPS:	Throughout this story, George is rhyming nearly everything he says in a style similar to Dr. Seuss. This story also includes a lot of audience involvement and would work best with a large group of listeners.

    Since Bonnie will be directing the volunteers onstage, she will need to be very familiar with the script before the skit begins. This is one skit that might be best for teen leaders or adults to read. Perhaps the teacher could do Bonnie's part and a student could do George's.

    In the script, wherever ellipses (. . .) occur in the narration sections, pause and allow the audience volunteers enough time to do the actions.

    The storytellers could be either boys or girls. Both readers start onstage or enter together. Bring up the stage lights and then begin when the students are quiet.

Teacher: **Lights! . . . Camera! . . . Action!**

Bonnie: **OK, today's story is about a lady named Tabitha, and we're going to use some audience members to help tell this story.** *(Search the audience for a guy to play the role of Peter. Then point to him and continue)* **OK, you be Peter. Let's have you step over here to the left side of the stage.**

George: **He be Pete.**

Bonnie: **Right.**

George: **Pete he be.**

Bonnie: **Um . . . right.**

George: **Would you like to play with me?**

Bonnie: **What are you doing?**

George: **I will rhyme.**

Bonnie: **That's nice.**

George: **All the time.**

Bonnie: **OK.**

George: **Because I know it's not a crime.**

Bonnie: **Look, just wait with your rhyming until we start. Stand over there while I get some other people to help us with this story.**

George: **I will stand.**

Bonnie: **Good.**

George: **On the land.**

Bonnie: **Oh, great.**

George: **Would you like to shake my hand?**

(Bonnie goes through the audience, choosing the remaining seven volunteers: two people to be the "doorway," two girls to be "weeping widows," two people to be the "disciples," and a large boy or a man to be Tabitha. For fun, give Tabitha a wig

to wear. As you assign the people their parts, say something like . . . "OK, you be the doorway and you be the weeping widows . . . you two be the two disciples . . . and you be Tabitha." Position Peter off to the left of the stage and the disciples off to the right of the stage; the rest of the people can begin on center stage.)

Bonnie: **Once, long ago, there was a lady who lived in Joppa,**

George: *(Pointing to the man playing the part of Tabitha)* **He be she.**

Bonnie: **And her name was Tabitha.**

George: **She be he.**

Bonnie: **Right.**

George: **That be one big girl, you see. Hee, bee, jee, bee, jee, bee, jee.**

Bonnie: **And she would make clothes** *(Pause, and, if necessary, encourage Tabitha to pretend to sew)* **and give them away to the poor.**

George: **I be poor.**

Bonnie: **You can stop that now.**

George: **Poor I be. Would you give some clothes to me?**

Bonnie: **OK, so one day Tabitha got sick.** *(Pause and give Tabitha time to act sick. Remember, before continuing to read any of the parts, make sure the volunteers have completed the actions)*

George: **She be sick.**

Bonnie: **Really sick . . .** *(Allow Tabitha enough time to act sicker)* **. . . Even sicker . . .**

George: **Sick she be.**

Bonnie: **That's enough already.**

George: **Please do not throw up on me.**

When Tabitha Got Sew Sick . . . She Dyed

Bonnie: She got so sick, she died . . . She fell to the floor and her friends—that's you, weeping widows—washed her body . . . *(Pause and give the widows time to act this out. If appropriate, say, "Just hose her off or something . . .")* And carried her to an upstairs room . . . *(Pause again. Let them struggle with carrying Tabitha!)* They opened the door . . Go ahead, push the door open . . . and set her inside . . .

George: *(As they carry her away)* She be dead. Dead she be. Do not drop that girl on me.

Bonnie: When they found out that Peter was in a nearby city, they sent two disciples to go and get him . . . Don't forget to close the door! . . . They told Peter, "Come at once!" . . . So, Peter went with them back to Joppa . . .

George: Wait a minute . . . Why did they do that if she was already dead?

Bonnie: Well, they knew that with God's power, anything is possible.

George: You mean, they wanted her raised back from the dead?

Bonnie: It sure seems like that's what they were thinking.

George: Whoa.

Bonnie: So then Peter and the disciples arrived in Joppa and all the ladies stood around crying . . . When Peter arrived, they took him upstairs to the room where Tabitha was lying . . . They opened the door . . . And walked inside . . . and all the women were sitting around crying . . . and looking at the clothes Tabitha had made while she was alive . . . and then Peter—

George: —He be Pete. Pete he be. He not be as dead as *(Point to Tabitha)* she.

Bonnie: As I was saying, Peter sent the women and the men out of the room . . . Don't forget to close the door . . . And then, he got down on his knees . . . and prayed . . .

Bonnie: Finally, he turned to the dead woman and said, "Tabitha, get up!" . . . She opened her eyes . . . looked up at Peter . . . and sat up . . .

George: She be back! Back she be! She not be so dead you see!

Bonnie: And Peter took her by the hand . . . and helped her to her feet . . . He opened the door . . . took her downstairs to the rest of the people . . . Don't forget to close the door . . . and everyone was amazed! . . . Let's give all our actors and actresses a great big hand for a job well done!

George: They done well. Well they done. And we had a lot of fun.

Bonnie: *(After the volunteers have returned to their seats)* Well, *(insert the name of the other storyteller)* _____, do you know what this story can teach us today?

George: Well, *(insert the name of the other storyteller)* _____, it shows us that God is more powerful even than death. And we can talk to God about every problem we have, even things that seem impossible for us to do on our own.

Bonnie: You got it. Good job!

George: *(As they exit)* Hey, next time can I be Pete?—I be Pete. Pete I be. Would you eat green eggs with me?

Bonnie: I know what author your momma used to read to you when you were a kid.

George: Do you know? Is it so? Was it Edgar Allen Poe?

Bonnie: Um . . . No . . .

Together: The end.

(Bow. Fade out the stage lights. Exit.)

When Tabitha Got Sew Sick . . . She Dyed

The Broken Jail Jailbreak

(Paul and Silas)

BASED ON: Acts 16:16-36

BIG IDEA: God miraculously released Paul and Silas from prison.

BACKGROUND: Paul and Silas, two missionaries in the early Christian church, were traveling around preaching the gospel when a slave girl began to follow them. The girl was possessed by a demon that could predict the future and her owners made lots of money through this special ability of hers. After Paul and Silas set the girl free from the demon, the girl's slave owners had them arrested.

God orchestrated a way for them to be released from prison and to witness to the jail's warden and his family.

CAST: Two storytellers, one who reads the parts, the other who leads the actions.

PROPS: None

TOPICS: Angels, conversion, demons, faith, freedom, God's power, ministry, witnessing

DIRECTOR'S TIPS: For this storymime script, it might be helpful if the person doing the actions has some experience in mime, theater, or just likes acting goofy. The storytellers could be either boys or girls.

With this type of storytelling one person serves as the primary storyteller and the other person does the actions or shows the emotions of the characters and events in the story. The speaking storyteller pauses after every action verb to allow time for her partner to act out what's happening in the story. Suggested actions are included.

Invite the audience to imitate, or "mime," the actions after the silent storyteller has performed them. This is a great way to include audience participation and works especially well with five- to ten-year olds. When doing this, just remember to have your reader wait long enough for the children to perform each action before continuing reading the next section.

The storytellers could be either boys or girls. Both readers begin onstage or enter together. Bring up the stage lights and then begin when the students are quiet.

STORYTELLER 1	STORYTELLER 2
Paul and Silas, two missionaries, were walking along the road one day.	*Walk in place. Make up a goofy walk.*
And a slave girl began to follow them.	*Shrink. Walk like a girl.*
She was possessed by a demon.	*Act demony.*
That helped her predict the future.	*Wave your hand in front of you. Ta-da!*
Now, her slave owners made lots of money by having her predict the future.	*Weigh some money in your hand. You're a slave owner and you love that money.*
For days and days she followed Paul and Silas wherever they went.	*Walk back and forth quickly. You're following someone everywhere.*
She was telling everyone that Paul and Silas knew the way to be saved from sin!	*Two thumbs up. It's good news.*
But Paul and Silas didn't want a demon interrupting them all the time so they were getting really annoyed.	*You're really annoyed!*
Paul told the demon to go away.	*Turn your thumb to the side, flick it through the air. Get out of here Mr. Demon!*
And it did.	*Wipe your brow. You're relieved.*
But, without the demon, she couldn't predict the future anymore.	*You're totally confused. You can't predict the future!*
And since her slave owners could not make any more money they were furious!	*Make a mean, angry face.*
They grabbed Paul and Silas!	*Grab an imaginary person in front of you.*
And convinced a crowd to beat them up.	*Beat up the imaginary person.*
And then they chained them up and threw them in prison.	*Chain up an imaginary person and shove him into prison!*
Finally at midnight,	*Howl like a wolf.*
(To the other storyteller; you're annoyed) **There were no werewolves there.**	*"Oops."*
But at midnight, they heard a loud sound.	*Loud noise!*
It was an earthquake!	*Shake! You're in a quake!*

The Broken Jail Jailbreak

Well the chains around their ankles fell away and they were free!	*Jump up and down. Huge smiles. Do a little dance.*
The prison shook and all the jail doors flew open.	*Shake and then throw open the prison doors.*
The jailer thought all the prisoners were going to escape and he started to freak out!	*Freak out. You're scared!*
But Paul told him no one escaped, and he calmed down.	*Relax. You're cool, happy, at peace.*
He remembered that the girl had told everyone these men knew how to be saved.	*Tap your head. You remember something important!*
He ran up to Paul and Silas and asked how he could get saved.	*Fold your hands. Plead!*
They told him to trust in Jesus and he would be saved.	*Now, fold your hands in prayer. Look up to heaven.*
So he did. And so did his family, and they were all baptized!	*Duck down, then stand up like you just stepped out of the water. Hands high, you're happy!*
Then the jailer put bandages on Paul and Silas's wounds.	*Put bandages on an imaginary person next to you.*
Then they had a great big party to celebrate!	*Throw up your hands. Celebrate! Party!*
So, in the end, Paul and Silas were set free from prison.	*Break out of handcuffs.*
The girl was set free from a demon!	*Wipe your brow. You're relieved.*
And the jailer and his family were set free from sin!	*Arms in the air! Cheer!*
The end.	*Take a bow.*

The Broken Jail Jailbreak

A Couple of Cool Heroes
(Priscilla and Aquila)

BASED ON: Acts 18:1-28; Romans 16:3, 4; 1 Corinthians 16:19; Ephesians 6:21, 22; Colossians 4:7-9

BIG IDEA: Priscilla, Aquila, and Tychicus aren't as famous as some of the other Bible characters, but they're heroes in God's eyes because of their faithfulness and courage in sharing the gospel with others.

BACKGROUND: As the early church grew, new converts needed to be mentored by mature believers. Priscilla and Aquila, two people whom many Bible scholars believe were married, trusted in Christ. They became friends with the apostle Paul; helped train the early defender of the faith, Apollos; risked their lives to protect Paul; and hosted a church in their home.

Tychicus is also referred to in this story. Paul refers to him as "a dear brother, a faithful minister and a fellow servant in the Lord" (Colossians 4:7). These three Bible heroes can serve as a great inspiration to believers today. This short skit will help remind your students that it isn't fame that makes someone a hero in God's eyes, but rather faith.

CAST: Bonnie—A slightly more serious storyteller trying to tell the story (girl or boy)
George—Her friend, who occasionally gets things mixed up (boy or girl)

Note: These names are used only for the purpose of clarity in the script. You may wish to use the actual names of the two storytellers as you present the story.

PROPS: None

TOPICS: Courage, faithfulness, God's Word, leadership, ministry, witnessing

DIRECTOR'S TIPS: The readers could be either boys or girls. Both readers start onstage or enter together. Bring up the stage lights and then begin when the students are quiet.

Teacher: **Lights! . . . Camera! . . . Action!**

Bonnie: **You know,** *(insert the name of the other storyteller)* **_____, sometimes the Bible lists heroes of faith who are still well-known even today.**

George: **Right,** *(insert the name of the other storyteller)* **_____; like Moses or Abraham or Peter or John the Baptist.**

Bonnie: **But there are also lots of people mentioned in the Bible who aren't very well known at all, but are still heroes in God's eyes.**

George: **Because of their faith in him and their faithfulness in spreading the good news about Jesus.**

Bonnie: **Right. For example, Paul mentions a guy named Tychicus.**

George:	**Did you say, tickle us?** *(Tickle Bonnie)*
Bonnie:	**No! Not tickle us!**
George:	**OK, tickle you.** *(Tickle Bonnie again)*
Bonnie:	**Tychicus! His name was Tychicus. And Paul calls him "a dear brother, a faithful minister and a fellow servant in the Lord."** [1]
George:	**He sounds cool.**
Bonnie:	**He was cool. He also encouraged the believers, delivered messages for Paul, and spread news among the early Christian churches.** [2]
George:	**Very cool. Oh, I know about a couple of other Bible heroes who aren't that famous, but were still faithful!**
Bonnie:	**Who are they?**
George:	**Priscilla and Aquila! And they really were a couple of church leaders.**
Bonnie:	**Do you remember which one was the guy?**
George:	**Aquila.**
Bonnie:	**And who was the woman?**
George:	**Priscilla.**
Bonnie:	**Very good.**
George:	**Yup, and it's cool how their names kinda rhyme.**
Bonnie:	**Right.**
George:	**Priscilla and Aquila. Say it with me.**

Bonnie:	**I'd rather not.**
George:	**Priscilla and Aquila. Go on.**
Bonnie:	**No thanks.**
George:	**Priscilla and Aquila. C'mon.**
Bonnie:	*(Sighing)* **Oh, all right. Priscilla and Aquila.**
George:	**Priscilla and Aquila and Attila the Hun.**
Bonnie:	**All right, that's enough.**
George:	**Priscilla and Aquila ate a vanilla gorilla.**
Bonnie:	**No, they didn't. But they did have a church that met in their home.**
George:	**In their villa.**
Bonnie:	**They risked their lives for Paul,**
George:	**And trained a brilliant Bible scholar named Apollos.**
Bonnie:	**Even though we don't hear about them all that much today, they're famous in God's eyes.**
George:	**So, you don't have to be well known to be a hero in God's eyes?**
Bonnie:	**Nope. Not at all. Just keep believing,**
George:	**And following Jesus.**
Together:	**The end.**

(Bow. Fade out the stage lights. Exit.)

[1] Colossians 4:7
[2] Ephesians 6:22, 22; Colossians 4:7–9

A Couple of Cool Heroes

SCRIPTURE VERSE INDEX

TOPICAL INDEX

The First Christian Martyr (Stephen)
Preacher to the World (Paul)

Forgiveness
The Day Sin Came In (The Garden of
    Eden)
Final Forgiveness (Joseph—Part 3)
Rappelling Through the Roof (Jesus
    Heals a Paralyzed Man)
The First Christian Martyr (Stephen)
Preacher to the World (Paul)

Freedom
Flaming Foliage and Major Plagues (The
    Plagues)
The Unlikely Hero (Gideon)
The Man Who Slept in Graves (Jesus
    Heals a Demon-possessed Man)
The Broken Jail Jailbreak (Paul and
    Silas)

Friendship
The Sons of Thunder (James and John)
Rappelling Through the Roof (Jesus
    Heals a Paralyzed Man)

Generosity
When Tabitha Got Sew Sick . . . She
    Dyed (Tabitha and Peter)

Giftedness
The Woman Warrior (Deborah)
The Real-life Superhero (Samson)
The Giant Match-up (David and Goliath)

God's Existence
The World's First Artist (Creation)
The Barbeque on Carmel Mountain
    (Elijah)
The Man Who Ate Grasshoppers (John
    the Baptist)

God's Love
The Day Sin Came In (The Garden of
    Eden)
The Guy Who Wouldn't Kiss Mrs. Potty
    (Joseph—Part 1)
Unidentified Flying Angels (Jesus' Birth)
The Sons of Thunder (James and John)
At the Scene of the Grave (Jesus'
    Resurrection)

God's Power
The World's First Artist (Creation)
The Flood (Noah)

Flaming Foliage and Major Plagues (The
    Plagues)
God's Spy Guy (Joshua)
The Unlikely Hero (Gideon)
The Giant Match-up (David and Goliath)
The Barbeque on Carmel Mountain
    (Elijah)
The Man Who Slept in Graves (Jesus
    Heals a Demon-possessed Man)
Nets of Fish (The Miraculous Fish
    Catch)
Rappelling Through the Roof (Jesus
    Heals a Paralyzed Man)
When Tabitha Got Sew Sick . . . She
    Dyed (Tabitha and Peter)
The Broken Jail Jailbreak (Paul and
    Silas)

God's Sovereignty
Dungeon of Dreams (Joseph—Part 2)
Final Forgiveness (Joseph—Part 3)
The Kayak Kid (Moses)
The Dutiful Daughter-in-law (Ruth)

God's Word
The Day Jesus Stayed Behind (Jesus at
    the Temple)
The Man Who Ate Grasshoppers (John
    the Baptist)
Preacher to the World (Paul)
A Couple of Cool Heroes (Priscilla and
    Aquila)

Grace
The Day Sin Came In (The Garden of
    Eden)
At the Scene of the Grave (Jesus'
    Resurrection)
Preacher to the World (Paul)

Grief and Loss
The Dutiful Daughter-in-law (Ruth)
When Tabitha Got Sew Sick . . . She
    Dyed (Tabitha and Peter)

Holy Spirit
The Unlikely Hero (Gideon)

Hope
The Courageous Beauty Queen (Esther)
Unidentified Flying Angels (Jesus' Birth)
The Man Who Ate Grasshoppers (John
    the Baptist)
The First Christian Martyr (Stephen)

Idolatry
The Barbecue on Carmel Mountain
    (Elijah)

Jealousy
The Guy Who Wouldn't Kiss Mrs. Potty
    (Joseph—Part 1)

Jesus
Unidentified Flying Angels (Jesus' Birth)
The Day Jesus Stayed Behind (Jesus at
    the Temple)
The Man Who Ate Grasshoppers (John
    the Baptist)
The Man Who Slept in Graves (Jesus
    Heals a Demon-possessed Man)
Nets of Fish (The Miraculous Fish
    Catch)
The Sons of Thunder (James and John)
Rappelling Through the Roof (Jesus
    Heals a Paralyzed Man)
At the Scene of the Grave (Jesus'
    Resurrection)

Leadership
Final Forgiveness (Joseph—Part 3)
The Woman Warrior (Deborah)
The Real-life Superhero (Samson)
A Couple of Cool Heroes (Priscilla and
    Aquila)

Listening
Flaming Foliage and Major Plagues (The
    Plagues)
Unidentified Flying Angels (Jesus' Birth)

Ministry
The Man Who Ate Grasshoppers (John
    the Baptist)
Nets of Fish (The Miraculous Fish
    Catch)
The First Christian Martyr (Stephen)
The Broken Jail Jailbreak (Paul and
    Silas)
A Couple of Cool Heroes (Priscilla and
    Aquila)

Miracles
The Barbecue on Carmel Mountain
    (Elijah)

New Life
The Man Who Slept in Graves (Jesus
    Heals a Demon-possessed Man)
At the Scene of the Grave (Jesus'

Resurrection)
Preacher to the World (Paul)
When Tabitha Got Sew Sick . . . She
 Dyed (Tabitha and Peter)

Obedience
The Day Sin Came In (The Garden of
 Eden)
The Flood (Noah)
Flaming Foliage and Major Plagues (The
 Plagues)
God's Spy Guy (Joshua)
The Daring Outcast (Rahab)
The Dutiful Daughter-in-law (Ruth)

Patience
Dungeon of Dreams (Joseph—Part 2)

Passover
Flaming Foliage and Major Plagues (The
 Plagues)

Peter
When Tabitha Got Sew Sick . . . She
 Dyed (Tabitha and Peter)

Planning
God's Spy Guy (Joshua)

Priorities
The Day Jesus Stayed Behind (Jesus at
 the Temple)
The Sons of Thunder (James and John)
Rappelling Through the Roof (Jesus
 Heals a Paralyzed Man)

Prophecy Fulfillment
Flaming Foliage and Major Plagues (The
 Plagues)
Unidentified Flying Angels (Jesus' Birth)
At the Scene of the Grave (Jesus'
 Resurrection)
The First Christian Martyr (Stephen)

Purpose
Dungeon of Dreams (Joseph—Part 2)
The Kayak Kid (Moses)
The Woman Warrior (Deborah)
The Unlikely Hero (Gideon)
The Dutiful Daughter-in-law (Ruth)
The Barbecue on Carmel Mountain
 (Elijah)
The Courageous Beauty Queen (Esther)
The Day Jesus Stayed Behind (Jesus at
 the Temple)
The Man Who Ate Grasshoppers (John
 the Baptist)
Nets of Fish (The Miraculous Fish
 Catch)
Preacher to the World (Paul)

Questions
The Guy Who Wouldn't Kiss Mrs. Potty
 (Joseph—Part 1)

Rebellion
The Flood (Noah)

Repentance
The Barbecue on Carmel Mountain
 (Elijah)
The Man Who Ate Grasshoppers (John
 the Baptist)

Resentment
The Guy Who Wouldn't Kiss Mrs. Potty
 (Joseph—Part 1)
The Unlikely Hero (Gideon)

Rest
The World's First Artist (Creation)

Second Chances
The Day Sin Came In (The Garden of
 Eden)
The Flood (Noah)
Flaming Foliage and Major Plagues (The
 Plagues)

God's Spy Guy (Joshua)
The Real-life Superhero (Samson)

Sin
The Day Sin Came In (The Garden of
 Eden)
The Flood (Noah)
Nets of Fish (The Miraculous Fish
 Catch)

Success
The Woman Warrior (Deborah)
The Unlikely Hero (Gideon)
The Real-life Superhero (Samson)
The Giant Match-up (David and Goliath)

Suffering
The Guy Who Wouldn't Kiss Mrs. Potty
 (Joseph—Part 1)
Dungeon of Dreams (Joseph—Part 2)
Final Forgiveness (Joseph—Part 3)
The Kayak Kid (Moses)

Temptation
The Day Sin Came In (The Garden of
 Eden)

Vengeance
The Real-life Superhero (Samson)

Witnessing
Unidentified Flying Angels (Jesus' Birth)
The Man Who Slept in Graves (Jesus
 Heals a Demon-possessed Man)
The Sons of Thunder (James and John)
The First Christian Martyr (Stephen)
Preacher to the World (Paul)
The Broken Jail Jailbreak (Paul and
 Silas)
A Couple of Cool Heroes (Priscilla and
 Aquila)

Worship
Unidentified Flying Angels (Jesus' Birth)

27 Won't You Be My Neighbor?

Look It Up

Based On: Luke 10:25-37

Big Idea: We need to love others by showing compassion to everyone (not just to the people we'd prefer to love).

Life Application: Every one of us has failed to show the kind of love for others (and for God) that God's Word requires. Rather than try to justify ourselves (like the lawyer in this story tried to do), we should admit our shortcomings and then ask God to forgive us and help us to live lives of genuine compassion.

Topics: Compassion, following God, God's Word, mercy, obedience, prejudice

Background: An expert on Jewish religious law asked Jesus how to receive eternal life. Jesus pointed him to the Bible's commands of loving God and our neighbors perfectly.

Instead of realizing that he hadn't done that, the guy then tried to justify himself before Jesus. He was looking for a loophole! He asked Jesus, "OK, then, who *specifically* is my neighbor?"

This is not just a story about being nice. Jesus' story of "The Good Samaritan" was meant to pull the rug out so this guy wouldn't be able to justify himself—so that he'd realize his need to ask for and receive God's forgiveness!

When we retell this parable to our students, we can try to accomplish the same two things Jesus did: (1) reveal to our students that they haven't kept God's law perfectly, and (2) give them a guide on how to live the way God desires.

With God's help, we can understand how we've failed to live his way, and—through the power of his Holy Spirit in our lives—we can begin to act in sync with God's will.

This is the story of "The Good Samaritan."

One day, a man was _____ along the road when he was attacked by a group of
(a verb ending in "ing")

_____!
(a dumb occupation, plural)

They beat him up and took his_____! They even took his
(a noun, plural)

_____!
(something a woman wears)

He was hurt so bad all he could say was "_____!"
(a weird saying)

Then they tossed him in the ditch and went on their way.

Well, pretty soon a _____ came along. Now, of course, the guy expected him to help
(a very important occupation)

him. But instead, the _____ just said "_____!" and went on his way!
(the occupation from the previous blank)   *(a saying from a TV show you don't like)*

Later on, a _____ came _____ along the road. When he saw the
(an occupation you wouldn't want)   *(a verb ending in "ing")*

hurt man, he just said, "_____!" and left him there.
(a way to say goodbye in another language)

At last, a man from _____ came along. The hurt guy hated people from
(a state or country you don't like)

_____! He hated them so much he used to call them _____!
(the state or country from the previous blank)   *(an insult)*

So you can imagine how surprised he was when that guy _____ for him
(something nice you might do for someone, past tense)

and helped him! He poured _____ on his sores and then _____ his
(a gross liquid)   *(a verb, past tense)*

wounds. Finally, he took him to a nearby _____ and paid for his stay!
(a hotel chain)

And Jesus said we should go and do likewise, even to the people we like to call

_____.
(another insult)

The end.

Act It Out

Cast: You'll need 6–8 children to act out this story:
INJURED MAN (boy), 1–3 ROBBERS (boys or girls), PRIEST (boy or girl), LEVITE (boy or girl),
SAMARITAN (boy or girl), DONKEY (preferably a strong adult)

Props: None

Tips: This is an easy story to act out. It's action-packed and familiar. Have fun, just make sure the
ROBBERS don't get too carried away during the beating-up part!
     You may wish to have a strong adult play the part of the DONKEY because people ride
on his back!

**Starting
Positions:** Position onstage the INJURED MAN in the center, the ROBBERS on the left, and everyone else
on the right. Bring up the stage lights, and then begin when the listeners are quiet.

Discussion Starters:

*The context is vital to understanding
this parable. Be sure you spend some
time discovering who Jesus told
this story to (a religious expert) and
why Jesus told the story (so the guy
couldn't justify himself before God).
(See Luke 10:25-29.)*

*How does this story apply to us
today? Do people ever try to justify
themselves before God today? What
does this story have to say to them? In
addition, what does this story teach
us about loving others? How will
studying this story change your life
this week?*

End with prayer.

A man was walking along the road . . . when he fell into the
hands of some robbers! . . . They attacked him! . . . They beat him up
really bad . . . and even stripped him of all his clothes—but we'll just
use our imagination for that part . . .

They left him on the ground, half-dead . . . (I said they left him.
They didn't keep beating him up!) . . .

A priest was going along the same road . . . He saw the man,
but passed by on the other side with his nose in the air . . . A Levite
came along too . . . but he also passed on the other side, whistling to
himself . . .

Then a Samaritan came along . . . riding on his donkey . . . He saw
the man, got off his donkey . . . and helped him . . . He put medicine
on the guy's wounds . . . all of his wounds . . . *ALL* of 'em! . . . Then he
bandaged him up . . . and put the guy on his donkey . . . Then they
rode to an inn where he cared for him . . .

The end.